God and Other Men

Praise for God and Other Men

"Myrna Smith refused to conform to anyone's rules as she explored the wisdom of extraordinary teachers around the world. Her quest to find God leads her to the universal common denominator of peace, which is love."

— Lo Anne Mayer
Author, *Celestial Conversations:
Healing Relationships After Death*

"Myrna Smith's story assures every seeker, skeptic, and student of truth that there's virtue and treasure in the looking."

— Gary Renard
Author, *The Disappearance of the Universe*

"Never has Myrna Pershall Smith accepted trite or dubious solutions to her soul's deepest yearnings. The result is a lifetime of tested and practiced wisdom, culled from all the great philosophical traditions of the world and the hard-won lessons of her own heart. This book tells the whole tale in language that never veers from the elegant."

— Elizabeth Gilbert
Author, *Eat, Pray, Love:
One Woman's Search for Everything
Across Italy, India and Indonesia*

God and Other Men

Religion, Romance, and the Search for Self-Love

Myrna J. Smith

Foreword by
Seijaku Stephen Reichenbach, Roshi

CAPE
HOUSE
CAPE HOUSE BOOKS
ALLENDALE, NEW JERSEY

GOD AND OTHER MEN
Religion, Romance, and the Search for Self-Love

Copyright © 2013 Myrna J. Smith

ISBN-10: 1939129044
ISBN-13: 978-1-939129-04-8

Cape House Books™
P.O. Box 200
Allendale, NJ 07401-0200
www.CapeHouseBooks.com

Cover and book design by Bill Ash

Extracts from the Authorized Version of the Bible (The King James Bible), the rights in which are vested in the Crown, are reproduced by permission of the Crown's Patentee, Cambridge University Press.

Excerpt from "Live" from LIVE OR DIE by Anne Sexton. Copyright © 1966 by Anne Sexton, renewed 1994 by Linda G. Sexton. Reprinted by permission of Houghton Mifflin Harcourt Publishing Company. All rights reserved.

Some names and identifying details have been changed to protect the privacy of individuals.

Cataloging in Publication Data

Smith, Myrna J.
God and Other Men: Religion, Romance, and the Search for Self-Love / By Myrna J. Smith; Foreword by Seijaku Stephen Reichenbach, Roshi.

p. cm.

ISBN-10: 1939129044
ISBN-13: 978-1-939129-04-8

1. Spiritual enlightenment — search for 2. Spiritual teaching — religious aspects and beliefs 3. Religion — Western 4. Religion — Eastern 5. *A Course in Miracles* — teachings of 6. Memoir — family life

BM 645.P7L87 2013
158.1208 Pe

For my children

Thad, Stephanie, and Elaine Smith

Table of

Contents

Foreword

God and Other Men is a road map for the authentic spiritual journey of the heart and includes its triumphs and failures, agonies and ecstasies.

By its nature spirituality is relational. A person's fullest potential cannot be realized without relationship. Love completes us. Whether it be love for God, ourselves, or another, we cannot claim freedom or enlightenment unless we have learned the lessons exclusive to love.

Like spirituality, love is not about some destination but about the journey itself. All the sacred teachings are fully realized in a commitment to loving-kindness which alone can set us free from the containment in which we do so much of our living. What's important is that we love and never stop loving regardless of whether we ever know the joy of the love of another. When we are given love, we must realize it is not for us to keep but to be shared in order that we and others may grow and be completed.

The journey is lifelong, often arduous, and certainly mysterious, but it is one we must take if we ever expect to know who we truly are, who God truly is, or enter Nirvana, or the Kingdom.

We do not get to choose who we love. All the great masters have called us to love "all the many beings however innumerable they may be" and to "love them as we love ourselves." But we can only give what we have. Therefore, it must go that love begins with loving ourselves so that we may love and be loved by others. As Rumi once wrote, "It is not our work to find love but to remove all of the mental and emotional barriers we have built within ourselves preventing us from seeing it everywhere."

This is the spiritual journey, one we can choose to take or not to take, but if we don't we will never have a feel for the fullness of life. This is the path of the spiritual warrior, the seeker, the master, and the student. So let's get about the journey, one step in front of the other, again and again and again. This is life's invitation and its full meaning.

Foreword

In these pages Myrna Smith has given the reader hope and proof that the journey is the destination. The reader will recognize this story in a way they recognize a friend in a crowd because it is your story, my story, the Buddha's, Christ's, and that of anyone who has ever made the journey to find themselves, their purpose, and the essence of life we call Love.

—Seijaku Stephen Reichenbach, Roshi
www.seijakuroshi.org

Seijaku Roshi is the author of *Kokoro, The Heart Within: Reflections on Zen Beyond Buddhism*. He is the founder of The Zen Society in Shamong, New Jersey.

CHAPTER 1

Gary's Leaving

*a*s I stepped into the kitchen that cold, dark Sunday night in February, I noticed immediately that two chairs were missing from their places around the kitchen table. Though I wasn't surprised, I felt a tightening in my heart as if I had to brace myself for what was to come. I had been skiing with my son and two daughters that weekend and was eager to feed them and get them to bed. I didn't have the courage to check the rest of the house before finishing the bedtime routine. The rituals helped calm the rising anxiety that flowed through my body. My husband of seventeen years had moved out of the house that weekend. I had told him to take whatever he wanted.

Once the children were in bed, I investigated missing items more thoroughly: two chairs from the dining room; one television, the small one; and two paintings, one with flying ducks, given specifically to him by the mother of his high school friend, and one of clowns, painted by a colleague of mine. He'd taken the case of his grandmother's hardly used silverware, which we'd displayed prominently on the counter next to the dishwasher. It was just silver plate, not real silver. I preferred stainless steel, anyway. Also gone were a few kitchen tools—a wine opener I liked, a spatula, and a can opener. He took some dishes and two pots. Surprisingly, he left half the Fostoria crystal glasses his mother had passed on to us as well as a white vase that had been a wedding present from one of his professors.

When I opened his office door, I couldn't help being jarred by the emptiness of the room. Gone were his desk, the bureau, and the bed he used as he gradually moved more and more of himself into his office and out of our bedroom. I opened the closet and ran my hand along the cool pipe that had held his clothes. I left the room and made my way down the hall to check the closet there. The familiar smell of leather from his black and white high school letter jacket did not greet me. The closet was half empty. Each discovery of something missing in the house expanded the emptiness in my heart.

Though I had longed for intimacy, as I suspect Gary did, we had had no idea how to achieve it. In the evenings, after the children went to bed, we usually sat across from each other in the living room and read the local newspaper. I would sit on our green couch, he in the chair opposite me. They were the only two places with good light. We would discuss the news, read each other interesting tidbits from the paper, and maybe Ann Landers or a good bridge hand. We would exchange information about his office politics, my students. The arrangement was pleasant, homey, but not intimate: we never discussed our discontents with each other so they spread like crabgrass, entangling all aspects of our lives.

I sat on the green couch around 8:30 and had finished the paper by 8:40. After all, it wasn't *The New York Times*. Then I wandered again, wishing I had formed habits like listening to music or watching television, but neither of us had allowed these enjoyments to become part of our lifestyle. We had focused on reading, writing, and studying, and we both embraced silence. But without him shuffling through papers near me or in his office, the silence felt oppressive. No streetlights lit my country road, and neither Gary nor I had fixed the outside house lights. The intense darkness added to my sense of isolation.

What was I going to do the rest of that evening and all the evenings to come? I could read a book or prepare for the English classes I taught, but I didn't have that level of concentration. Besides, time was not really the problem. What or who would fill the capacious void in my chest? I saw a terrible loneliness stretch out before me like railroad tracks I had once observed as a child. Then, like now, I wondered: will they go into eternity?

My thoughts turned to an earlier period in my life when someone else I loved had moved away. When I was 14 my paternal grandmother moved from eastern Oregon, where we lived, to Portland, where her daughter, my aunt, lived. Until then, Grandma had lived less than a quarter of a mile from our house in a simple, tiny home. Inside those three rooms I found companionship and unconditional love. She taught me all kinds of card games, including casino, canasta, and pinochle. But mostly we played cribbage. I loved pegging around her old cribbage board and was proud to beat her if I could. We listened to soap operas on the radio, mainly *Stella Dallas* and *Young Widow Brown*. She often made pancakes, even for dinner, a treat for a child whose mother always served vegetables. I used to tell her, "I love you up to the sky and back," something I never said to either of my parents, and she replied with some alternative like, "I love you up to the moon and back."

Grandma. This picture was taken in 1911 when she was 28. My father would be born three years later.

I didn't mind her primitive outhouse, a two-holer, with the Montgomery Ward catalog for toilet paper. Nor did I mind looking at the tar paper, sometimes in tatters, on the sides of her house. What I saw, and what stays in my memory, were the beautiful morning glories that grew high and wide, covering half the house with blue blossoms. Growing anything required effort in that high desert: crops grew courtesy of water collected in mountain reservoirs and released through a series of canals and ditches constructed during President Roosevelt's New Deal. Grandma had a well from which she pumped water for the flowers and her house. Every year she grew those heavenly blue morning glories with their yellow throats and brought color to that brown and black house in that brown and gray expanse.

Sometimes on a summer evening we would sit in front of those morning glories and watch lightning strike in the mountains that surrounded our valley. Grandma would say, "How far away is that lightning strike?" I would count to ten or even fifteen before we heard the crackle of thunder. Then I would divide by five, giving a rough estimate of our distance from the strike. It was never near enough to be threatening. I felt secure there.

Grandma didn't leave all at once. From time to time she took the bus across the state to stay with her daughter and then return. But the day came when she didn't. I have no memory of that event. I only know it happened. I know my reaction to her leaving only because my aunt told me of a letter I wrote to Grandma in which I pleaded with her to return because I couldn't live without her.

Within the first year of her leaving, our family made a trip across the state to visit her and see her new living quarters—a small house next to the service station my aunt and her husband operated. They lived in an apartment above the station. On the long drive I sat in the back seat and dreamed of what it would be like to see Grandma again. I thought how wonderful it would be to bask once more in that perfect acceptance and love. *Maybe we could even play some cribbage*, I thought to myself. Somehow I couldn't imagine that her attention would not be focused on me.

Almost sixty years after that event, I still remember walking into that little house with great expectations that were immediately dashed. She hardly noticed me; her focus was on her own oldest child, my father. During the entire stay I didn't get a chance to spend any time with her alone.

I felt rejected by her, so I returned the favor and carved her out of my conscious life. I saw her when the family gathered, and she came to my wedding, but seeing her no longer made my heart tingle.

I found relief, as I always have, by being successful in my school or academic life and by having either a best friend or boyfriend. Gary grew up twelve miles from me. Our parents knew each other because both his and my paternal grandfathers had struggled to make farms out of the desert when the Works Progress Administration put in the irrigation projects. Our grandfathers, along with their grown sons, had had to tear out the native sage-brush and cheatgrass to plant wheat, barley, and alfalfa. I didn't see Gary, however, until our elementary schools played basketball in eighth grade, and I didn't meet him until our freshman year in high school. We were immediately interested in each other and had our first date before the end of the year.

We married our junior year in college, just before our twenty-first birthdays. I still wasn't close to my parents, and I felt that without him I would be completely alone in the world. In some ways we were a good match. We were both committed to success because of our families. His father had

With Gary in Las Vegas on our honeymoon in 1961.

become a self-made cattle rancher and moved far beyond Gary's grandfather's financial accomplishments. My parents, true children of the Great Depression, had remained poor. My father scratched out a living, farming only sixty-five acres and later working as the janitor for the local school. Gary wanted to replicate his father's "success." I wanted to escape my father's "failure."

Gary and I did well in college, well enough to continue graduate studies in the Midwest. For those first five years we had a strong marriage, mainly because we kept our common focus on success. After academic jobs in Wyoming, we moved to New Jersey where he landed a job with a pharmaceutical company and I with a community college. In a few short years we achieved the American dream: three beautiful children, a house on four acres, two cars, a dog, a horse, and parties with our social group almost every weekend.

But every day I felt the cracks that had formed as soon as we finished graduate school—the breakdown in communication, our vague angers and resentments. We never openly fought. We just picked away at each other for the smallest of sins. I couldn't stand it if he chewed gum around me. He became annoyed if I left a crumb on the counter or failed to polish the cooking pots. I couldn't bear the way he criticized the kids; he couldn't bear my "hippie" friends. Our life reminded me of a shiny, Red Delicious apple still on sale in the grocery store long after the season: it looked great, but it was mushy under the skin and rotten at the core.

Eventually Gary and I tried marriage counseling, a pointless exercise because the rift between us was too deep by the time we went. Besides, he already had made the decision to move back to his parents' cattle ranch, back to the brown desert. Although my parents still lived near his family, I did not seriously consider moving, not that he ever asked me directly. To me, the place was bleak, dry, soulless.

The all-encompassing loneliness I felt that first night on the green couch was not a stranger to me. It had appeared before. When I was twelve or thirteen, three horror stories appeared in *Reader's Digest*. My father read them and talked about them at the dinner table, piquing my interest. Always wanting to impress my father, I read them in one day. In "The Specialty of the House," a chef and restaurateur serves his special dinner once every couple of months to a select group of friends he is fattening up to become the next specialty of the house. At the end of the story the restaurateur walks out with his next victim, "patting his meaty shoulder."

Neither that story nor William Faulkner's "A Rose for Emily," with its murder and necrophilia, put me over the edge, but Shirley Jackson's "The Lottery" did. Jackson writes about the citizens of an American town who annually stone to death the person who "wins" the lottery. In the story a young wife and mother wins, and even her children participate in the stoning. The senseless, random evil touched me in some deep place. I felt as if I were in a dark hole. I slept during the day, not wanting to eat, and felt despondent.

My next round of darkness came when Gary and I temporarily broke up during our junior year in high school. The night we broke up, I went to my bed, lay on my stomach, and cried. Though I tried to muffle my sobs with my pillow, my parents must have heard me. Daddy came to my bedside and patted my back. "Gary and I broke up," I sobbed.

"That must be what divorce feels like," he responded in a comforting voice.

Even though my father made me feel better that night, neither of my parents said anything to me the next day or the next week, and I didn't volunteer more information about the breakup or my pain. I didn't want to expose my vulnerability. That depression lasted until Gary and I made up a month later.

Three years before our separation, I taught some of the poems from *Live or Die*, Anne Sexton's book, to an evening class of mostly adults. We ended the class on the poem "Live" in which the pull Sexton felt toward the forces of life—her husband, two daughters, and the birth puppies she didn't drown—appeared to have won out over

self-mutilation and death. She ends the poem on
this happy note:

> *Just last week, eight Dalmatians,*
> *¾ of a lb., lined up like cord wood*
> *each*
> *like a*
> *birch tree.*
> *I promise to love more if they come,*
> *because in spite of cruelty*
> *and the stuffed railroad cars for the ovens,*
> *I am not what I expected. Not an Eichmann.*
> *The poison just didn't take.*
> *So I won't hang around in my hospital shift,*
> *repeating The Black Mass and all of it.*
> *I say Live, Live because of the sun,*
> *the dream, the excitable gift.*

The students and I felt certain Sexton had overcome her worst demons and would live. But she
didn't. She killed herself a few days after that class,
and some dam within me broke, allowing blackness, flowing like water, to engulf me. For three
days I felt lost. Had I chosen to teach Sexton's
poetry because I, like her, felt on that precipice
between life and death? Had I, like her, felt that a
husband, children, success, and friends were not
enough? Did we both have a void in us that the
world could not fill?

No one in my family suffered from depression.
If they did, they had not spoken of it. I recognized
its symptoms mainly from Emily Dickinson's po-

ems in which she calls depression "an imperial affliction" or, in contrast to my blackness, "that white sustenance, despair."

I still carried out my roles, as my Puritanical upbringing and marriage had so deeply trained me to do. But I moved like a robot. Living seemed pointless. I couldn't work up any feeling for my friends, children, or work because the darkness dominated my mind.

On the third day of my depression, a Saturday, Gary and I stood in our kitchen, which had been painted bright orange. I began cleaning out the dishwasher. While handing him pots, I began, "I have been feeling depressed." I tried to look at his good eye; the other one, damaged in a childhood accident, usually wandered. I thought, *Can he see me? Can he see my pain?* He said nothing. I bent over to pick up the bowls and felt their smooth surfaces. I finally said to him, "If this blackness continues, I will have to kill myself."

Without a moment's hesitation, he replied, "Don't you dare leave me with these three kids."

The comment did not encourage me to talk further. In fairness, I had not communicated how seriously the condition affected me. After all, we did not talk about our feelings, especially dark ones. When I woke up the next day, the black had lifted for no logical reason. Perhaps some part of me recognized that I had to rescue myself. Or perhaps just speaking that little bit of dark truth had freed me.

William Styron speaks of incomplete grieving being a contributor to depression in his book *Darkness Visible: A Memoir of Madness*. He believes the death of his mother when he was thirteen contributed to his depression. Certainly I had not grieved openly or consciously when Grandma moved. My parents didn't help me and may not have even known about my suffering. I have always been good at masking negative feelings. Though my first round of depression occurred before Grandma left, something happened to my psyche when she did. That next year I gained twenty pounds and I began hating my parents, something that lasted well beyond normal teenage rebellion.

I began therapy after my Anne Sexton depression. I didn't see then, as I do now, that the emptiness inside me, manifested as depression, had been with me all my life. When Grandma moved, it had intensified. Little events, like reading stories or poems about evil or death, or big events, like Gary leaving, brought the emptiness forward. Going from Grandma's arms directly into Gary's arms had contributed to my inability to work out the difficulties with my parents. Had Gary not filled the void Grandma left, I might have been desperate enough to talk with my parents about my fears and loneliness. If I had been able to communicate with my parents, maybe I would have been more equipped to work things out with my husband.

Why I had such difficulty talking to my parents, I am not sure. I frequently felt like the odd person out. All the family liked to take their ease. No one was in a rush to do anything. None of the other children studied hard enough to be a straight-A student, as I was. Except in the spring, when crops had to be planted in a timely way, Daddy took a nap during the day. Often he would return from the morning chores, or sometimes after lunch, and lie down on the tweed living-room couch and sleep for twenty minutes. He did his work dutifully and skillfully, but ambition, especially for money, eluded him.

No matter what else my mother did during the day, she took at least forty-five minutes to eat every meal. She rarely ate sweets and died thin, but she relished every meal. She sewed most of our clothes and ironed for everyone, but she did everything at her own pace—slow. My three siblings had the capacity to enjoy our parents' pace. Not I.

When I was still in primary school, Daddy read an article about phrenology. He felt the bumps in all of our heads, and sure enough, I had more bumps than anyone else. "Ambition bumps," my father declared, and that was not a compliment. By first grade I decided to be the best student (or best anything) and didn't give up on that goal until many years later.

As long as my grandmother lived next door and gave me recognition and love, I didn't notice that my parents didn't seem to care about my report card. After she left, I felt more and more estranged from them for vague reasons: they didn't give me enough attention; they loved my older sister and younger brother more; they were not materially successful. Even as I resented them, I wanted their recognition and praise. They never gave it, probably because they didn't think I needed it. After all, I received lots of recognition in school. Once in high school, I kept earning A's with the exception of a B+ in Algebra II. The teacher wrote on the report card, "This should have been an A, but Myrna talks too much."

When I showed my father the report card, he walked into the kitchen, grabbed a pen, and wrote, "You should hear her mother." He didn't say one word about my grades.

Though I dutifully called my parents regularly throughout my life and visited them every couple of years, we spoke about safe subjects and enjoyed each other's company by playing the family card game, pinochle. I talked to them about my successes but never shared my sorrows. When I called and alerted them to the separation from Gary, I know they blamed me and those "ambition bumps." Referring to my career, my father once said, "It seems as if you want to be a man."

So when Gary and I separated and I still didn't have my parents' understanding or support, I felt more isolated than ever. In retrospect, I see I didn't want them to know I needed support. I didn't want anyone to know about the crack in my psyche that could open into a wide crevasse if someone so much as stepped on the weakened snow of my heart.

Over the next few years, the loneliness I felt that first night after Gary moved out became less poignant: I organized my life to avoid its sharp edges. I moved one of my children into what had been Gary's office, bought a new small television for my room, and even watched it occasionally. I no longer spent long evenings on that green couch, though I did spend many hours on the black or brown couches of several psychotherapists.

I also did what my family members and millions of others all across the world have done when they found the world lacking and their own hearts empty. I began looking for a spiritual path. If I could not find happiness as a wife, mother, and professional, maybe I could find it in religion.

CHAPTER 2

Family Business

My family provided numerous religious paths to follow, which was one of the reasons it became so difficult for me to choose one. Religion dominated my family; it was the family business. I, however, wanted the family to be in real business or at least find a way out of poverty.

From my paternal grandfather's family I learned about Emanuel Swedenborg, a seventeenth-century Swedish mystic. In his fifties Swedenborg experienced dreams and visions and believed God had made it possible for him to visit heaven and hell and talk with angels and demons.

That side of my family featured a horse thief, a murderer, a syphilitic, and a schizophrenic, so religion lost out to more demanding activities. Nonetheless, I received what my paternal grandfather passed down—a belief in the importance of having one's own experience with God.

In the 1940s, my grandmother, who only finished third grade, and my father, whose education stopped after high school, read books by an Indian, Yogi Ramacharaka. They'd belonged to his grandmother. It'd be another twenty-five years before Westerners traveled en masse to India to learn from the Hindu gurus. Yogi Ramacharaka gave my father two ideas he clung to his entire life: reincarnation and karma. Emmet Fox, the New Thought spiritual leader, called the latter "the law of retribution," making karma more palatable to Judeo-Christian readers.

Grandma began reading the works of Charles and Myrtle Fillmore, the founders of the Unity School of Christianity. An early feminist, Grandma particularly liked Myrtle Fillmore's book, *How to Let God Help You*, not only for its content but because it was written by a woman. Her well-worn copy of Charles Fillmore's book, *The Twelve Powers of Man*, went to my father when he cleaned out her house and to me when we cleaned out his. Grandma subscribed to the *Daily Word* for herself and to *Wee Wisdom* for Lynette and me and any other grandchildren who passed through her house. It contained games and jokes as well as metaphysical lessons.

Grandma also owned a copy of the *Bhagavad Gita*, the ancient Hindu text. A small, blue copy, ragged at the corners from generations of reading, now sits on my bookcase. She read the Bible and the *Daily Word* regularly, along with the Hindu books of her mother and pamphlets written by great teachers such as Joel Goldsmith and Lillian DeWaters. Grandma's name, Vida Pershall, appears in some of the books and pamphlets I now own. It is written in her childlike hand: her parents and teachers made her write with her right hand, though she clearly favored her left.

My aunt, the one to whom my grandmother fled, became a serious student of Joel Goldsmith, taking courses from his students, listening to his lectures, and reading his books. Goldsmith, a Christian Science healer who felt too constrained by his church's focus on physical healing, founded his own organization, The Infinite Way. When, at age eighty, that aunt moved out of her house and into assisted living, she shipped all the Goldsmith books and tapes to me.

Daddy, not as taken with Fillmore or Goldsmith as Grandma, studied Emmet Fox, especially his book, *The Sermon on the Mount*. Fox's interpretation of what he believed to be the central teaching of Jesus appealed to him. Fox's main point, summarized in his discussion of the first beatitude,

"Blessed are the poor in spirit; for theirs is the Kingdom of heaven," is that we must give up our desire for self will in the search for God. We must become poor in our individual spirit to join the Spirit of God or the Kingdom of Heaven.

Many of Fox's pamphlets, such as *The Golden Key*, *Keeping a True Lent*, *Reincarnation: Described and Explained*, *The Four Horsemen of the Apocalypse*, and one that I read in a desperate moment as a teenager, *Alter Your Life*, came into our house. Fillmore and Fox reinforced for Grandma and Daddy the idea of Jesus as teacher, but not savior.

Daddy also discovered Edgar Cayce in the 1940s when he read the initial magazine article in *Coronet Magazine* and *There is a River,* the book by Thomas Shugrue that made Cayce famous. Later he joined the Edgar Cayce society (Association for Research and Enlightenment) and remained a member for more than thirty years. He bought and read many of the books written about the famed psychic. Cayce, through his trance readings, gave health advice to sick clients. To others he revealed past lives, causing him to embrace the idea of reincarnation. Yet Cayce attended the Presbyterian Church his entire life and read the Bible in its entirety every year, a practice he started at age ten. Cayce was a model for Daddy: he did not have to reject the teachings of Jesus to believe in reincarnation.

My mother, whose family members were traditional Christians, took my three siblings and me to the local nondenominational (read evangelical) church, which we always called Sunday school because sometimes we had no minister and, therefore, no church service, just Bible classes. The Sunday school building, located on a corner of our parents' property, resembled our family's houses — bare boards exposed under torn tar paper. With parishioners like us, where would the church get money for paint or siding?

The church had a piano, though, and a small stage where we children acted out the Christmas story every year and where Mr. Kremer, the first minister, pranced back and forth as he urged us, Sunday after Sunday, to get off the fence and accept Jesus Christ. I can still hear him: "You are either on the side of God or the side of the devil." In the winter the woodstove and Kremer, as my father contemptuously called him, heated up about the same time. His face got red and his fat belly bounced out of his suit jacket — he always dressed up to preach — as he piled on reasons, mostly built on fear, for us to choose Christ and be saved.

Sometimes, especially in the evening service, Kremer would place a bench on the stage and have an altar call, meaning he asked people to come forward, kneel, confess their sins, and be saved. In the winter people had to keep on their coats to go to the bench because it was so far away from the stove in the back of the church. One day Betty, a girl in my class wearing a gray and green wool coat, went forward, and I wondered whether I should also have gone. As I watched her kneeling at the bench, I wanted to feel the joy she felt—perhaps she might have called it ecstasy—but I never went. Grandma and Daddy used to say everyone would be saved, so I didn't have to proclaim it.

Many sermons from Kremer or the other ministers who passed through the church resembled the description of the last days in James Joyce's *A Portrait of the Artist as a Young Man:* Jesus and God, with his white beard, sit in a stadium with those of us who had been saved as we watch the burning and screaming of those who hadn't. Daddy and Grandma always said we created our own hell, so even at a young age, I could listen to those horrible sermons with detachment, which turned to contempt when I was about twelve. I also doubted whether Mother believed in that kind of hell, although she would not criticize Kremer or the other ministers because she felt duty bound to make her children into good Christians.

In addition to Sunday services and an occasional Wednesday night prayer meeting and altar call, each summer my mother sent us to Daily Vacation Bible School, so I knew the Bible stories well. One Sunday, as my mother and I sat in the second or third row on those hard pews, Kremer asked during the sermon, "What happened when John baptized Jesus in the Jordan River?" Never wanting to pass up an opportunity to show how much I knew, I piped up, "A dove flew down and God said, 'You are my beloved son in whom I am well pleased.'" I heard gentle laughter from the audience and felt blood go to my face. I knew I had the right answer. Kremer even incorporated my response in his continuing sermon, so why had people laughed? I had expected recognition, not ridicule. I never found out whether the minister had posed a rhetorical question or if the congregation was surprised by such a young child spouting out the response, but it added one more item I could hold against that church.

Daddy refused to attend. He had consented to being baptized before being married, but only at my mother's insistence. The issue of faith remained a lifelong struggle between them. Oddly, she did not insist that any of her children be baptized. Maybe forcing my father's baptism took the fight out of her. Years later, during a trip to Israel, my sister Lynette and I baptized ourselves in the Jordan River, along with Lynette's husband and a Jewish friend. We did it at the very spot the dove spoke to Jesus.

I was an official Christian long before that baptism, however. The summer I was seven and Lynette nine we attended, as usual, Daily Vacation Bible School. Our two younger siblings, Michael and Davida, must have attended also, but Lynette

was the one to whom I was most bound. The teachers, sent by some governing body, lived in the
community for just those two weeks. Two young
women, hardly more than teenagers themselves,
came to our community to teach that summer. Each
night they ate dinner with a different family from
the church. When they arrived at our house Mother
sent the four of us across the highway to pick peas
for supper. Daddy had planted the peas next to the
barley so he could irrigate the two crops together.
Nothing grew without irrigation, and, unlike
Grandma, we had no pump in our yard. We took
brown paper bags our mother had saved—she
saved everything—to hold the peas. Squatting between the rows and picking peas in the still hot
field, we were a captive audience for these young,
ambitious-for-Christ women. When they started
talking about Jesus, I knew what we were in for.

First they asked us to pray, to thank God for the
food around us. Then the one with the dark hair
said, "You must invite Jesus in. He is just waiting
for an invitation. Say the words, 'Jesus, come into
my heart.'"

We said, in turn, "Jesus, come into my heart."
But Lynette and I both knew what was coming
next. They asked us to say the statement we had
avoided, a statement that was spoken over and
over again at Sunday school, a statement that Daddy and Grandma would find repugnant: "I accept
Jesus Christ as my personal savior." Had we been

closer to the house, we could have just run inside. But we were across the road so there was no escaping.

"You each have to say the words or they won't take," said the one with the freckles and long reddish hair.

Lynette (on right) and me at the family farm in Willowcreek, Oregon, circa 1943.

What were we to do? We had been trained to mind adults.

After we each had made our individual proclamations, "I accept Jesus Christ as my personal Savior," they clapped their hands. The darker one said,

"It is so wonderful. You are saved." Perhaps she pictured two new stars in her heavenly crown. Lynette and I tried to act happy too, but we knew in our hearts we had betrayed Daddy and Grandma.

When Mother was growing up, attending church had been her main activity because her tyrannical father would not allow her to attend any school functions where boys might be present. Instead of resenting church, as a rebellious teen might have done, she found solace there. She sang in a trio with her mother and one sister and, later in life, joined a choir and often led our Sunday school in singing. Mother didn't endlessly talk about religion like Grandma and Daddy did, so who could tell what she actually believed? She went to that little evangelical church on the corner of their property until all the children left home.

Then she insisted that Daddy drive her to town—she never learned to drive—to attend the Methodist Church eleven miles away. Maybe she felt they finally could afford the gas to drive to town. I know she had tired of hearing those same sermons on sin and eternal damnation and of the ubiquitous emphasis on being saved, but she still wanted the comfort of hearing the familiar words of the Bible and the hymns she sang as a child. Besides, she had to hold onto Christianity because of the religious struggle with my father. Or maybe it was her very identity to which she was clinging. After the children left home, she had a difficult time finding a rewarding role for herself. Going to church reminded her who she was—a Christian.

Being saved in the pea patch didn't take for me, although as a tween I lived a divided existence: karma and reincarnation at home, fire and brimstone at church. By the time I went to high school I refused to go to church with my mother and would have liked to flee from my father when he started talking about reincarnation and the law of retribution. But we lived in a three-room house. After my grandmother moved, I had no place to go.

Daddy did try to live what he believed. He paid his debts, got along with all the neighbors, and rarely criticized anyone, except for their religious beliefs. Once our family went to a J. C. Penney store to shop for school clothes. The store featured overhead cables through which cash, placed in cylindrical containers the size of a soup can, moved from a clerk to a central location where an important person could make change. The containers made a swishing noise as they passed overhead. We picked out items for each of us kids. I suppose I got new socks and underwear, but what I remember were two new striped tee shirts I could wear to school with my jeans. Daddy chose a new felt hat that he immediately put on his head. He gave the clerk the money, and she sent it swishing up to the second floor. The container came back with the change, and we left.

While walking out to our car, I noticed Daddy didn't say much. He was thinking about the bill. Just as we reached the car, he said, "I don't think they charged me for the hat." He looked at Mother, probably for support, and continued, "I better go back and pay for it. If I don't pay for it now, I will have to pay later. And it might cost a lot more." Much to my amazement, because I knew how poor we were, he went back and paid.

I had become aware of being poor the summer I turned six, the year Daddy built a living room, bedroom, and bathroom—no more winter trips to the outhouse—onto the one room we'd all shared.

Lynette and I had almost no toys, so we improvised. We played elaborate pretend games with blankets, empty boxes from the kitchen, and, that summer, discarded building materials. From the shingles, Daddy cut us little pieces of cedar about an inch wide and three inches long. He drilled a hole in the top for a string so we could make them into necklaces. Lynette and I decorated our new jewelry by pasting a small ball of cotton onto the wood and we wore our necklaces proudly—until we went to town. Eleven miles away, the town contained about twelve hundred people. Still, we didn't get to go often, so Lynette and I took advantage of every opportunity to see the world.

Daddy had to go to the dentist—he was being fitted for dentures—and he told the two of us to stay near our old pickup. Those were the days before we upgraded to a used car. We tried to stay out of the hot Eastern Oregon sun and obey him, so we sat on the running board wearing our bibbed overalls, tee shirts, high-topped brown shoes, and

Lynette, Mother, and me with the old pickup truck.

our beautiful necklaces. Along came a boy wearing nice pants and regular shoes. He asked about our clothes, especially our shoes and pants. I recall him being more curious than ridiculing though his comments about our clothes made us self-conscious. Suddenly, his tone changed.

"What are those things around your necks?" he asked.

"Necklaces," Lynette said. She always did the talking for us in difficult situations.

"They don't look like necklaces to me," he countered.

Suddenly, I saw our jewelry differently. When we went home, we discarded our treasures. That day the boy planted a seed of shame in me. It grew. By high school, it was in full bloom. When I was a freshman, I had so wanted a Jantzen sweater for Christmas, but that popular brand cost too much. My parents gave me a less expensive sweater. I felt too ashamed to even mention my Christmas gift to my friends. To make matters worse, Gary, with whom I had just begun flirting, received a red Jantzen sweater from his parents.

I also longed to go on a real vacation, not just a trip to visit relatives. Lynette and I weeded onions for seventy-five cents per hour the summer after my freshman year in high school. We pooled our money so our family could spend one night at a cabin on the lake in McCall, Idaho. I still remember diving from a little boat to swim, trying and failing to water-ski, but enjoying being pulled around the lake on a buggy board. At least I could tell my friends, "Yes, our family went to McCall for vacation."

Poverty did not seem to be such a horror to the other family members. It surely must have bothered Daddy, the breadwinner, but he kept his focus on religion and the supernatural. In 1956 he went right out and bought *The Search for Bridey Murphy*, both the book and the record—a true extravagance—and told everyone who would listen that the story, about a woman remembering a past life in nineteenth-century Ireland, proved reincarnation was truth.

But stories about Edgar Cayce readings reigned supreme. Over the dinner table Daddy summarized the readings. He spoke about the Egyptian past lives of some of the people associated with the Cayce group and about the cures that appeared in the books and magazines he read. In one, Cayce prescribed almonds, resulting in the shrinkage of one man's cancerous tumors. I thought contemptuously, *Why doesn't he stop reading about this ridiculous stuff, and concentrate on making money?*

By the time I left home to attend college, I wanted nothing to do with religion, mainly, I think, because I connected it with poverty. I tried to escape both poverty and religion by marrying Gary, a potentially successful man, and studying diligently to become successful myself. I didn't think beyond material success and romantic love. I wasn't yet twenty-one and I thought I was finished with my family's business, but I understood so little of what my spirit would demand.

CHAPTER 3

A Spiritual Community

For the five years after Gary and I divorced—I was in my early forties—I dabbled in religion and sought out spiritual groups. At first I stayed with ones that were at least nominally Christian because they felt familiar. Maybe some part of the Sunday school sermonizing and the pea patch pledge had stayed with me. I rejected mainstream Christianity though, with its emphasis on Jesus dying for our sins. God wanting a sacrifice from his son didn't fit with the God of my father and grandmother. My grandmother had regularly read the Bible, especially the Psalms and the Sermon on the Mount, to me and my siblings. Over and over, we heard the same phrases: "Be still and know that I am God;" "The meek shall inherit the earth;" "I am that I am;" and "The Lord is my Shepherd; I shall not want."

In my young mind the Hebrew Bible and the New Testament blended into one. When Grandma recited her favorite part of Psalm 91, with its reference to God's feathers, I saw myself safely curled up under an extremely large chicken that I associated with Jesus. There I was, only my head sticking out at the edge of a straw nest, as I waited for Grandma to work up to a final crescendo.

He that dwelleth in the secret place of the most High shall abide under the shadow of the Almighty.

I will say of the Lord, He is my refuge and my fortress: my God; in him will I trust.

Surely he shall deliver thee from the snare of the fowler, and from the noisome pestilence.

He shall cover thee with his feathers, and under his wings shalt thou trust: his truth shall be thy shield and buckler.

(Authorized Version of the King James Bible)

Just the sound of that last, completely unknown word "buckler" sent chills up my spine. That was the God I wanted—not the bird, the protector. I wanted a God who could heal my own "noisome pestilence." A God who would take me back to the safety I felt with my grandmother.

I started looking in an extremely unlikely place—a Unitarian Church in Princeton, New Jersey, forty-five minutes from my home. A friend of mine attended and told me of the impressive sermons the minister gave. After I heard one, I looked forward to the next week. They were like great college lectures. I even took notes.

Another attraction: that church held a singles event every Friday night. Maybe some of those single men also went to church. What better place to meet a man? Certainly I would never go to a bar. Two reasons prevented me from going to the Friday night singles parties. First, my children often needed rides to their own events on Friday nights. Second, if I went, I actually would be admitting that I might want or need a date. I preferred my long-standing pattern of keeping my needs hidden. Besides, mingling with strangers was not my strong suit. Better to just go to church and hope.

I didn't make new friends, however. Not men or women. Acquaintances, yes, but not friends. The long drive, after all, limited my participation in many of the church activities. Nor did the services satisfy my spiritual longings. The emphases were social justice, psychological issues, and the environment. It was my desire to belong to something that spurred me into joining. I looked forward to the ceremony and tried being particularly friendly to a man who had planned to join the same day I did. In the end, though, I didn't connect with the man or the organization. The Sunday I lit a candle and signed a paper, supposedly committing myself to that church, was the last time I entered the building.

My next attempt led me to Christian Science. My youngest child had a friend whose family had been in Christian Science for generations, and my conversations with the parents made me think I could find a home among Mary Baker Eddy's followers. Their belief that Jesus died to show that there was no death, and that spirit is the only reality, fell in line with the teachings of my grandmother and father, who believed the body was like a house and that the individual soul would move to new houses—bodies—through a series of deaths and rebirths as it lived out its accumulated karma. Jesus, in their minds, had solved all the human issues and, therefore, would not reincarnate; Jesus was the elder brother who came to show us the way. Although Christian Science did not embrace reincarnation, the idea didn't seem anathema to its fundamental teachings.

My main difficulty was this church's attitude toward medical treatment: most Christian Scientists go to Christian Science healers instead of doctors. Their reason for not seeking medical treatment stems from their belief about who we are. Our reality is spirit, made in the image and likeness of God, who also is Spirit. So a disease, they believe, must be an error.

I sensed a glitch in their logic: What about breathing and moving the physical body? Is that error also? Spirit surely doesn't need to eat or breathe. The mind-body problem is a question with which philosophers have wrestled for centuries. Are we a body, a mind, a spirit? If human reality is spirit, as the Christian Scientists say, then what is the meaning of our entire physical existence? Wouldn't all physical life itself be an error? But that question was too large for me to approach. After all, I just wanted a community that believed mostly as I did. I had a "craving for a community of worship" of which the Grand Inquisitor speaks in Dostoyevsky's *The Brothers Karamazov.* I put my feelings about doctors into the background with the hope those doubts would fade as my faith developed.

Most Christian Scientists I knew seemingly belonged to a tight-knit group and had great faith. Many had spiritual advisors. Because that all appealed to me, I started attending services and visiting Christian Science Reading Rooms. Mary Baker Eddy's *Science and Health* became my new Bible. Stories of dramatic physical healings, recorded in their publications and available in their reading rooms, fascinated me. In one story a woman who'd been hurt in a car accident began reading *Science and Health* instead of going to the hospital. She recovered, broken bones and all, in a few days. The stories were great.

Christian Scientists do not have ministers, but they do have healers and regional lecturers. I called a healer once for my bad back. She abruptly told me to read the creation story in the book of Genesis. Perhaps her advice was to remind me that I was spirit, not a back, but I was annoyed at being dismissed so quickly. She may have been so brusque because I didn't make an appointment and pay her, but I didn't want to pay for a healer. I had good medical insurance. The experience speaks of my tentative commitment to the ideas of Christian Science. I did, however, attend every special lecture held in the area for the six-month period I tried to join.

At the last Christian Science event I attended, the lecturer made a statement to this effect: "We shouldn't run a certain distance, not fifty laps or five miles. Rather, we should run to express the joy in living." At that point in my life I was swimming laps, trying to do thirty-six lengths of the pool a couple of times a week to strengthen my back. I did not like what I heard, but I saw the lecturer's point: swimming laps, or running five miles, was similar to getting a medical treatment. I thought to myself, *Christian Scientists do go to the dentist, and they do wear glasses, but they don't run laps or miles.* Splitting hairs over issues dealing with the treatment of the body was not for me. I never returned.

Men did take up some space in those first five years. I had a few romances, but none lasted more than a year. One man, the best sexual partner, left me. Another was too old. Another drank too much. Part of me really did not want a man to get too close because he would interfere in my relationships with my children. Yet the relationships with my children did not fill the emptiness in my heart. Each man distracted me from my loneliness—from that emptiness in the pit of my stomach, from that tightness in my chest—for a few months. The same can be said of my religious adventures. Was it a man I wanted, or was it God? I vacillated: religion or romance?

My next adventure took me out of Christianity and into Hinduism and the Indian guru system. That's when Ravi, who taught in the business department at my college, became my friend. He came from a Brahmin family who had settled in Rajasthan after barely escaping to India from Pakistan during the division in 1948. Though he never abandoned the traditional Hindu rituals, Ravi was interested in exploring any kind of spirituality. He even knew of Edgar Cayce.

Ravi, an unusually warm and charismatic person with wavy, black hair lived in contradiction. He dressed in impeccably pressed suits at our college, where informality was the norm. Students, especially females, flocked to his office. At his home, where he often entertained people who shared his spiritual interests, he wore elegant, usually white, Punjabi suits. He led meditations and let it be

Ravi.

known that he preferred the celibate life, but his charm still attracted women wherever he went. I liked going to his house, which always smelled of curry. After meditation, he sometimes served delicious Indian rice pudding flavored with cardamom. There I met Emily, a Tarot card reader, who would host me in India later in my life.

In India Ravi had belonged to Ananda Marga, a global spiritual and social service organization founded by Anandamurti, and had lived at the main ashram in Calcutta. Members of Ananda Marga often visited Ravi and attended his meditations. Male or female, they dressed in orange, the color for followers who have taken the vows of a *sannyasin*, a person who has given up worldly life. Ravi, who was divorced, did not wear orange because he had relinquished his vows when he married. One night, he gathered a group to listen to a missionary named Nirupama, a woman in her forties who worked mostly in the Philippines for Ananda Marga.

She stood in front of our small group and recounted her first meeting with Anandamurti, telling how he appealed to her not only because of his capacity to love and help the poor, but also because of his ability to read her past history, "like a tape running across my forehead." Then she uttered a line that pulled me in like a small fish on a big hook. "Ever since I made a commitment to Anandamurti," she said, "I have never felt lonely."

Never felt lonely. This is for me, I thought. I agreed when Ravi and Nirupama offered to give me the Ananda Marga mantra, whispered to me in secrecy. To make the evening even more powerful, Nirupama came home with me that night because her vows did not allow her to sleep in the same house as a man. Nor did they allow her to sleep on a mattress. Before she curled up on the carpet in the living room, she led me in a meditation.

The two of us sat on the floor, she in the lotus position and I with my back to the wall and legs partially crossed. Pausing between each statement, she began, "Focus on your breath. Watch the inhale and the exhale. Feel the air as it passes over the upper lip. Let the concerns of the world fall away. Let any worry float away. Inhale, exhale." As she continued with prompts, I felt myself go deeper and deeper into some kind of profound experience. Then she stopped the prompts and let silence reign. A feeling of oneness, described so often even in scientific books on meditation, came over me. The feeling resembled the afterglow of a satisfying sexual union with a beloved. I heard bells, smelled perfume, and lived in ecstasy for about fifteen minutes. Maybe this is what I was supposed to feel when I accepted Jesus as my personal savior in the pea patch. Within the week I was making plans to go to India.

Fortunately, my children lived with their father in Oregon for two or three months every summer. The arrangement was one of the unforeseen benefits of my divorce. Most mothers with growing children can't take a six-week trip to India.

I decided to first educate myself about the Indian guru system. A pandit, I learned, has an education but not necessarily followers, while a guru has followers but not necessarily an education. Swami

Rama, the founder of the Himalayan Institute, was the first guru I ever saw. His worldwide organization had a branch in Pennsylvania, just a two-hour drive from my house. I went for an all-day event that included a talk by Swami Rama and a meditation led by Pandit Usharbudh Araya. The institute, housed in a former seminary, featured beautiful grounds and a large building as well as smaller ones. That day nearly a hundred people came, mainly to see Swami Rama. What a sight he was—tall, handsome, confident, and powerful.

Although my memory of most things he said has faded, two remain clear. To encourage us Westerners to meditate, Swami used a quote from the Bible that my grandmother used to recite with quiet conviction, "Be still and know that I am God." He also said that most Westerners do not know how to meditate, that we tend to see meditation as "spacing out" while it's actually about achieving a high state of awareness.

Following the talk, Pandit Araya led the group in a moving and memorable meditation, though I didn't find it as powerful as the one with Nirupama. Like her, he emphasized focusing our attention on the breath. He gave prompts about our breath to keep us from spacing out and to deepen our experience. I would see Pandit Araya, now known as Swami Bharati, twenty years later at the Himalayan Institute in Rishikesh on yet another trip to India.

I was impressed with Swami Rama but not knocked out, like Ravi and Nirupama had been with their guru. His book, *Living with the Himalayan Masters*, is a romp through his discipline, power, and magic. The Menninger Foundation of Topeka, Kansas, studied Swami Rama's bodily functions when he first came to this country in the early 1970s. What they found changed, at least for those who accepted the study, the relationship between the body and the mind. Among other things, they discovered Swami Rama could stop his heart from pumping for seventeen seconds; produce different brain waves, including theta, the drowsy sleep waves, while fully awake; and effect a ten-degree temperature difference in adjacent parts of his hand, all under controlled scientific conditions.

Later I learned that one woman sued the Himalayan Institute, claiming it did not protect her when she reported Swami Rama's repeated sexual advances. She received a jury award of $1.875 million, according to the September 5, 1997 edition of the *Philadelphia Daily News*. In 1983, I knew nothing of this story.

Although I liked Swami Rama better than any minister or priest I had ever seen, I still thought Ravi's guru must be more special. About that time, I heard of yet another Indian saint, Satya Sai Baba, a guru with millions of followers worldwide.

Through a connection in the Unitarian church, I located a couple who had become devotees of Sai

Baba, who was made famous by the miracles he performed. The couple gave me books about him and told me of the joy they experienced just being near him. He was best known for producing ash out of his hand, but he materialized many things, including rings and vases. On one of the couple's Indian visits to Sai Baba's ashram, a package of candy appeared in the lap of their daughter during *darshan*, which means "look" or "glance" and describes any change in consciousness resulting from an interaction between a devotee and a guru. Hindus believe a glance by a holy person brings special blessings to a person.

The couple told me Sai Baba groups exist in most states, including several in New Jersey, so I attended one with them, but nothing that occurred there moved me. Mostly, participants sang songs in praise of Sai Baba. The couple told me I absolutely had to see Sai Baba and gave me instructions on getting to his summer ashram outside Bangalore and for positioning myself in the crowd before *darshan*.

Ravi took me to visit yet another guru, who I will call Didi, the common name for women who have renounced their worldly possessions and responsibilities. Didi, who lived in Queens, had a hundred or so devotees in the New York City area and many in Calcutta and other cities in India. She had married and borne two sons before renouncing her worldly concerns and beginning to attract followers, mainly through her healing powers. On the day I saw her, she seemed like an upper middle class housewife reigning over a well-decorated home in a swank neighborhood. It belonged to her son, she said, because she, of course, had no possessions. Devotees from India filled the bedrooms. It is common for gurus and devotees to live together for weeks or even years at an ashram, a spiritual community, to provide opportunities for healing and instruction.

I presented Didi with two coconuts, a common Hindu offering. We had a pleasant visit and a typical Indian meal of rice, dal, and vegetables. She must have perceived me to be a serious seeker, or even a potential devotee, because she invited me to travel with her in August, the time we both would be in India. Didi asked Praity, one of her followers, a married woman in her thirties, if I could stay at her house in Calcutta. Praity agreed, so I wrote down her name, address, and phone number.

Although August was still months away, I assumed the devotee would remember the agreement. Ravi gave me instructions for locating Anandamurti's ashram. With plans in place to see two gurus, I felt all set for my spiritual adventure in India.

CHAPTER 4

India, 1983

I arrived in the early morning at the Delhi Airport in July when the thermometer often tips 100 degrees. The place teemed with Sikhs, Muslims, and Hindus, all in their distinctive clothing, most speaking languages I didn't understand. Ninety percent were men, many sporting beards, others brightly colored turbans. The pungent smell of curry filled the air. Baggage handlers and taxi drivers pressed themselves upon me for business. I felt anxious because of the foreignness, a feeling that grew when Ravi's older brother, who had agreed to meet me, did not. Nor did he answer the phone when I called. I hired a cab and drove to his house, located in a yellow, stucco complex of small houses and apartments surrounding a dusty open square. There I found him and his family just getting out of bed.

"We heard the phone, but we didn't want to get up yet," he said, unapologetically. On the other hand, he, his wife, and three young children offered me rice and dal, conversation, and a couch. It was extremely hot even by 10:00 a.m., but the fan cooled me as I drifted off to sleep.

Later in the day, Steve, a colleague of Ravi and mine who was traveling around the world, came to the home. I wondered where all of us would sleep. The apartment contained only a living room, kitchen, one bedroom, and a bathroom with only a hole in the ground and faucets for water. I didn't need to worry. In the evening they set up hemp cots in the garden. I hadn't slept under the stars since I was a kid and enjoyed a cool and pleasant rest.

Steve and I toured New Delhi and Old Delhi together, then moved on to Varanasi, the holiest city in Hindustan. All Hindus want to die there because death in that spot guarantees them a direct shot into heaven. Major streets lead to the Ganges River where ghats, wide, flat steps built down into the water, offer the morning faithful a walkway into the sacred river. Men strip down to their dhotis, a substitute for underwear, but women, who must stay covered, wear saris. They bathe, dunk their heads three times, and even rinse out their mouths with what they consider holy water from Mother Ganja. Upstream, people throw garbage, dead animals, dead children (only adults are cremated), and any number of pollutants into the river, but Indians maintain that the Ganges possesses a purifying quality that keeps the water safe, even allopathic.

In Varanasi, one can easily get lost in the narrow streets that lead to shops and homes. Smoke fills the air from both the dung fires used for cooking and the continual cremation fires that burn at specific ghats along the river. The sharp odors of turmeric, cumin, and other spices mix with the smoke, fill the nose, and stick to clothes. The heat and humidity made walking those narrow streets almost unbearable. Hawkers assault Westerners as prospective customers and hound them into buying products or at least visiting their shops. Child beggars tug on tourists' clothes and lepers show their decaying fingers.

Steve and I met up with a tourist group to do the required sunrise boat trip on the Ganges. No one would argue about the beauty of early sun on the river and the sight of practitioners coming down from their abodes for their morning ablution. But even there, hawkers in boats approached ours and began the drumbeat of "very good price" for items we didn't want at any price.

Steve, a gregarious person, invited our new group to come back to our small hotel for breakfast.

Even at that early hour everyone was hot and thirsty. Bottled water had not come into common use, so any drinking water had to be boiled. Evidently, our large group must have used up the boiled water because Steve and I both became ill within twenty-four hours. We had taken a train to Patna. Once there, we booked ourselves into a nicer hotel than usual because Steve felt ill. My illness exhibited itself less dramatically than his but lasted much longer. Three years later and twenty pounds lighter, a specialist in New York discovered I had both amoebas and Giardia.

But in Patna I felt only a little queasy. While Steve stayed near a bathroom at our hotel, I checked out the activities in and around the hotel and came upon a wedding parade. The groom, dressed in white, rode a small horse to the bride. She wore a traditional red sari and lots of gold jewelry. Most of the ceremony took place on the street, but the reception was held at our hotel. Typical of my experience with Indians, someone saw I was alone and invited me to join the party. I didn't feel like eating, but I was enjoying expanding my cultural knowledge. An attractive man standing near me asked, "Would you like to have something to drink?" I wondered what kind of drink he was talking about since Indians don't imbibe in alcohol. "Just come with me," he said in a charming voice as he led me to the elevator.

The minute he opened the door to the room, I realized I'd made a mistake. About thirty men, but not one woman, milled around the room. On a table with a white tablecloth was one bottle of VAT scotch and a few glasses. I should have left immediately, but I didn't want to appear ungrateful for the hospitality at the wedding. I stepped inside, the door closing behind me. At that moment, the lights went out. Within seconds I felt hands squeezing my bottom, rubbing my breasts, twirling my waist. Adrenaline pumped through my body and put me into flight mode. *Surely I won't get raped at a wedding. Not by Indians.* For a moment I thought that was a distinct possibility. *If I can just get into the hall, I'll be all right.*

The hands still groping me, I backed up until I felt the doorknob and opened the door just wide enough to slide into the hallway. Somehow I thought the lights would be on there, but they weren't. For a few minutes I remained panicked and ran down the hall, away from that room. But not one man followed me. By the time I found the stairs, the lights came back on and I made my way back to my room to check on Steve. Since he was still in the throws of illness, I kept my adventure to myself. I didn't want him to know how foolish I'd been.

In a couple of days Steve recovered enough to travel. We flew to Katmandu and spent a week there before he caught a flight to Singapore and I to Calcutta to begin the spiritual part of my journey.

In Calcutta, suitcase in hand, I went to the home of Praity, Didi's devotee, and knocked at the door. Something seemed strange, but Praity invited me in and offered me food. I concluded they did not know who I was: Didi had forgotten to remind them I was coming. I felt uncomfortable but did not want to embarrass my hostess. Praity, however, followed the Indian tradition and invited me to stay. Just as she was showing me my bed, her face brightened and she said, "I know who you are!"

The next day Didi arrived to great fanfare. The house was decorated with marigolds and special foods were prepared. Each devotee greeted Didi by bowing and touching her feet. Immediately she began tending to their needs, setting up appointments for the next few days. But every day she spent some time with me and her closest devotees in a relaxed atmosphere. Sometimes they sang *bhajans*—devotional songs—or just talked. Once they asked me to say a prayer of my religion. I recited the Twenty-third Psalm even though I didn't know what my religion was.

Both Didi and her devotees cautioned me not to go to the ashram of Anandamurti—I assumed that it was a matter of professional jealously—so I sneaked out one afternoon for a visit. Although I knew from Ravi's directions approximately where to go, I didn't know the organization had been outlawed by the Communist government of West Bengal. The taxi driver would not go too close to the ashram and dropped me a mile or so away. Feeling no fear, I flagged down a bicycle rickshaw to take me the rest of the way. I knew I was in the area when devotees, identifiable by their bright orange clothes, converged on one house surrounded by a five-foot-high stone wall.

I had been told by many Indians not to tip the bicycle rickshaw drivers too much or let them overcharge me, lest they come to expect the same from Indians. The driver asked for two rupees, but I did not have anything smaller than a ten-rupee note. Though the difference is pennies, the admonitions of my Indian friends, or perhaps my own parsimoniousness, made me look for change. Of course, the driver had none and certainly wouldn't admit it if he had. So I asked others around me.

Finally, a hand clutching two rupees came over the wall, and a woman speaking imperfect English said, "Here are two rupees. Just get out of the street before you get arrested." She was a German devotee of Anandamurti—tall, slender, about thirty. The previous week she had been arrested and held at the police station for a few hours, just for visiting the ashram. Once inside the compound I was safe, at least from the police.

A mixture of Indians and Westerners populated the ashram, about fifty in all. Also, half a dozen young men dressed in military uniforms and little green caps and carrying billy clubs walked about. *They must be here to protect Anandamurti from the police*, I thought. I didn't think much about them because I was intent on talking to people. I wanted to hear about their experiences with Anandamurti to see if they matched the wonders of which Ravi and Nirupama spoke. The Ananda Marga organization functions worldwide so many people have been influenced by this man. But my conversations did not go beyond Ravi. Some devotees remembered him, but not fondly. One disliked that he had married, another that he had not reciprocated his wife's devotion, saying, "She starved herself for him, but he didn't care. He didn't pay any attention to her." This puzzled me, making me wonder if there was a side of Ravi I didn't know.

"Why has Ananda Marga been outlawed here in West Bengal?" I asked one follower. Although I didn't get a clear answer, I found out Anandamurti had spent seven years in jail for murder.

"Trumped-up charges," the devotee said.

Just before Anandamurti made his appearance for *darshan*, the devotees stood respectfully and sang *bhajans* in Bengali. I did not join the singing. First, I had no idea of the words or how to pronounce them. Second, I wanted to focus on the guru. I felt as if I were about to meet a long-anticipated blind date. There was excitement in my heart. *Would Anandamurti have the same influence on me as he'd had on Ravi and Nirupama? Would I become a follower?* I already had accepted the initiation and often meditated with the Ananda Marga mantra.

Dressed in a long white robe decorated with gold thread, Anandamurti walked in. A select group of devotees followed. What a disappointment! No wonderful posture, no shining face, no magnificent smile, no visible aura, just a balding old man whose eyes looked a little bugged. *What had Ravi seen?* I wondered.

My disappointment quickly changed to fear when one of the guards came near me and poised his billy club over my shoulder. *Was I about to be arrested? Or hurt?* My heart pounded. Sweat dripped down my back. It was even hotter in Calcutta than it had been in Delhi. *Why had I come? Why hadn't I listened to Didi?*

The woman next to me, an American in her thirties, said, "He wants you to sing." I don't know what I sang, but my mouth began to move. Everyone around me looked at their guru with adoration and continued singing. Anandamurti didn't speak and only stayed for ten minutes before the guards helped him into a Mercedes-Benz and whisked him away.

After he left, I could hardly wait to escape. The German woman came to talk to me, "Come back in the evening. It is better because we can just be with Baba."

I wanted to say something sarcastic but merely said, "We'll see." Still shaken, I returned to Didi and her devotees without explaining where I'd been.

Each morning Didi woke up at three or four to meditate and pray for three hours, a process that seemed to bring her to the height of her powers. After breakfasting with Praity's family, she went to the room set aside for her and began seeing followers. They came to her for advice, healings, and blessings. I was not privy to their conversations, but I'd heard of past healings. One devotee had come to her for a skin condition that even affected her face. Didi told her to say certain prayers for fifty-one days. On the fiftieth day the devotee complained that her skin was unchanged. "This is just fifty days," Didi proclaimed. "I told you fifty-one." The next day, the woman's skin cleared.

Didi told me the story of a family — two brothers and their elderly father — who came to Praity's house for advice about their business. The father and his sons disagreed about how to run their affairs. She told them the father must retire and the sons should divide responsibilities in ways she defined. They left happy, ready to carry out her instructions. I couldn't imagine myself, or any American family, accepting the ruling of a religious leader on matters of business.

Didi's guru, a man in his seventies, came one evening to visit and eat a meal. He told me he usually didn't eat and lived just on sunshine and air. That day, to celebrate Didi being in town, he was making an exception. She was solicitous toward him and greeted him by bending down to touch his foot with her fingers, as her devotees did for her. She spoke to him respectfully, but her focus stayed with her own followers. He told me he had only four devotees and did not want more.

"Too much responsibility," he said.

That night we had a fabulous meal featuring more than twenty-five delicious vegetarian dishes, most of which I hadn't ever tasted. We in America hear about the horrible poverty in Calcutta, and I did see it. But I saw more wealth than poverty, primarily because of Didi's followers. Most belonged to a wealthy subcaste of merchants.

At such gatherings I spoke to Indians about their lives, especially their marriages. It seems this small subcaste had had difficulty matching their sons and daughters with appropriately wealthy partners. One extremely wealthy couple in their fifties seemed to have nothing to say: he was an intelligent man of the world, she a cloistered housewife. Though I saw them at several gatherings, I never saw them speak to each other. Their arranged marriage had produced one son named Bul. To find a wife for Bul they traveled as far as southern China in search of an Indian of their caste and wealth who had migrated there a generation or two earlier. The young couple had married shortly before I arrived.

The main problem for Bul and his wife was communication. His main language was Bengali, then Hindi, and finally English. Her primary language was Cantonese, followed by Mandarin, and then English. The three of us went to a Calcutta nightclub that had a lot of strobe lights but no alcohol. Consequently, it was dead and I spent the evening listening as the new couple struggled to talk to each other, mostly in English. It appeared they were falling in love though, and I hoped their marriage evolved into a more successful union than his parents apparently had.

I visited another couple, also Didi's followers, who lived in a large house with many apartments. The father owned the house and lived there with his six sons and their families. While each family had some private space, many rooms served all of them. Any money earned by the sons went to the father, who distributed it as he saw fit. The family had many servants and owned four cars, each with a driver. One of the daughters-in-law said there weren't too many conflicts in working out the schedule for the cars and common rooms. I asked Didi about the wealth of her devotees, and she responded bluntly, "Better to have wealthy ones than poor ones." As I recalled her lovely home in Queens, I couldn't have agreed more.

How did she acquire such wealthy devotees? I didn't have the nerve to ask. To be a guru has no requirements, except to have followers. "A guru removes the darkness," Didi told me. Maybe she had done a wonderful healing or cleared some hidden guilt for one member of this super-wealthy subcaste, and the others just fell in line. She didn't heal me, though, even after I asked for her help with the parasites I'd picked up in Varanasi. I didn't ask her to remove my spiritual darkness because I didn't want to become a devotee. I did, however, observe qualities I hoped to emulate.

Didi's ability to focus impressed me the most. One night in Calcutta her devotees sponsored a dinner at which she spoke. She sat in the front of the room in full lotus position. Devotees, also sitting on the floor in Indian style, filled the place. During the talk, conducted in Bengali, children ran around the room and made noise. They didn't distract her. She spoke to those followers as if she had a light that connected her to each of them. I knew I couldn't stay as connected to my students with so much commotion and realized Didi had a power I could not replicate and did not even understand.

When we were in the United States, Didi said she'd be traveling to south India. Because I enjoyed being with her and she invited me, I purchased a two-week airplane pass so I could make stops with her, see Sai Baba, and still get back to Delhi on the same ticket. When we left Calcutta, we ate at the airport because the plane was late. We didn't get the gourmet Indian food we'd been enjoying the last few days. I complained about the rice and dry vegetables. She responded firmly, "We like, we eat. We don't like, we eat." Since that day I've rarely complained about food.

On our way to her sister's house in Madras, now Chennai, we had two scheduled stops, one in Hyderabad, which we made, and one in Visakhapatnam. As we approached the latter, the pilot's voice came over the speaker, "Because of bad weather, we will not be landing in Visakhapatnam." My stomach tightened as I pictured a group of frustrated people waiting at the airport. In a worried voice I said to Didi, "What will we do? Your devotees will be waiting for you."

Didi, a woman in her fifties, twirled her finger in the air and said lightly, "God's will." In a moment her graying head slumped to one side and her hand, displaying a large red ring, lay relaxed in her lap. If she hadn't gone to sleep so quickly, I'm not sure I'd have been convinced of her perfect acceptance. That's a lesson on which I'm still working.

At her sister's house Didi became an ordinary person. She didn't get up early, meditate, or show that extraordinary strength I'd seen in Calcutta. Her older son, an international businessman, came to visit. She assured me she had no stronger feeling for him than she did for me, reminding me that gurus give up all personal relationships. But their intimate conversations about purchases and their knowing glances at meals made me suspect her assertion.

Didi purchased several items, including a two-foot sandalwood elephant she gave to Ravi's brother in New Delhi for safekeeping until I could take it to New York because she had too much luggage. Hers did not look like the life of a renunciate. Nevertheless, I felt it a great privilege to have been able to live and travel with Didi. Watching her gave me conflicting messages—great faith in the power of meditation, but little faith in the Indian guru system.

I'd hoped to find a guru for myself. I thought it'd be wonderful to be a part of a group that received spiritual guidance from an enlightened person. By the time I left Calcutta and had observed Didi, Didi's guru, and Anandamurti, I knew I didn't want to be anyone's devotee, but I still wanted to see Satya Sai Baba. Each of the gurus I had observed apparently had some extraordinary powers at specific times, but Sai Baba, according to everything I'd heard, lived in a constant state of grace and his powers were available at any moment.

CHAPTER 5

Satya Sai Baba

*a*fter spending a couple of days in Madras with Didi and her sister's family, I was ready to move on. They insisted I see the temples in Madurai and made arrangements for me to stay with a distant relative of theirs. I did what they wanted and visited the main temple, which covered an acre. The spectacular architecture and decoration outshone anything I'd seen, but part of me wanted out of the grip of Indian hospitality. Every day that I used my two-week pass meant a sacrifice of some part of my plans, and I didn't want to miss Sai Baba.

From Madurai I flew to Bangalore, in the state of Andhra Pradesh, where Satya Sai Baba has his summer ashram. Actually, the ashram is outside the town in Whitefield, but in 1983, Bangalore, now the Silicon Valley of India, could have been called Sai Baba City. His picture graced the wall or front desk of almost every hotel. The talk in the hotel lobby and restaurant revolved around him: "Are you going to *darshan*?" "What did he materialize today?" "Who got picked for a private interview?" Sai Baba enjoyed rock star status.

On that trip I saw him only once during a morning *darshan* along with five hundred others, mostly Indians. (From about 1990 to his death in 2011 thousands flocked to his every appearance so getting a seat anywhere near the dais at *darshan* proved difficult.) I sat under a large tent waiting for the great man to make his appearance. As instructed by devotees in the United States, I sat on the edge of a pathway so as to be close to Sai Baba when he entered. The crowd rustled and my heart quickened as he entered. He looked just like his picture: small body, orange garb, huge afro, and round, dark face. All turned toward him as he walked down the aisle, some hoping for eye contact, others pushing letters into his hand. Several men dressed in white, guards without billy clubs, followed closely behind him.

When he walked by me, I reached out and touched the bottom of his garment, hoping for healing like the woman in the New Testament who became whole when she touched the robe of Jesus. But nothing happened to me. I took this as a sign I wouldn't become a devotee and decided not to make the effort to go to *darshan* the next day.

The service was unimpressive. The group sang some *bhajans* and Baba spoke briefly in Telugu, the language of the region. My heart fell when I saw a red line between Sai Baba's lips, indicating he had chewed betel, a nut wrapped in a leaf favored by many Indians for its stimulant quality. I wanted him pure of any questionable habits or even physical enjoyments. Later, I read that Sai Baba defends the use of betel in one of the many books about him, saying, "The leaves, their juice, purify the blood. The nut digests."

Sai Baba is most famous for producing *vibhuti*, holy ash that comes out of his hands or appears on his pictures or other possessions of some devotees. On the day I visited, although I could not see clearly, the ash seemed to be coming out of Sai Baba's hand. A male, middle-aged attendant followed him around with paper towels so Baba could clean his hands after giving ash to the chosen.

Critics say he hides ash and objects in his sleeves, but both have appeared twice daily for more than sixty years in front of millions of people. Hundreds of books and many films have recorded Baba's many activities. Friends and acquaintances of mine have received materialized rings or pendants, which I have seen, most with a picture of Sai Baba on them, so I did not doubt he materialized the ash. I wasn't close enough, however, to see the process as precisely as I wanted.

The next day I was able to observe a Sai Baba miracle more closely when I visited a shrine dedicated to him in Mysore, a three-hour bus ride from Bangalore. The place was recommended to me by Sai Baba devotees in New Jersey. By this point the parasites I'd picked up in Varanasi made a surge in activity, so I didn't like going too far from a bathroom. Somehow that fear did not discourage me from taking pills and getting on an Indian bus and taking the hot, crowded ride to see a so-called miracle.

I had no address when I arrived at this ancient city. I simply asked a taxi driver to take me to the shrine of Sai Baba where the ash forms over his picture. Instantly the driver knew what I meant and took me to a small temple attended by just one man who spoke little English but knew what I wanted to see. He took me to a pint jar, half filled with a clear liquid. On the bottom lay an inch-long, flat, polished rock. He took out the rock, which had a picture of Sai Baba on it, and placed it in my hand. Liquid came out of the rock into my palm, as it had in the jar. He indicated I should drink it. It tasted sweet, like nectar. I did that several times before putting it back. The liquid is call *amrita*.

The story goes that the attendant, who built the shrine, had been a thief but became a changed man and a devotee when Sai Baba materialized this small rock for him. He built the shrine to demonstrate his devotion.

In addition to the stone, he owned a large picture of Sai Baba's head and shoulders but only the face showed because the rest of the picture was covered with ash, the same *vibhuti* that comes from Sai Baba's hand. The attendant encouraged me to brush some away, take it home to eat, or rub it on an achy muscle. I did. (Neither the nectar nor the ash cured my dysentery.) The attendant indicated with words and sign language that the ash would be back by the morning. I would have waited a few hours to see it forming, but I wanted to return to Bangalore before dark because I had a plane to catch for Bombay, now Mumbai, the original name before the British Raj.

On another longer stay in India in 2006, I saw the miracles of Sai Baba once again. At the end of that trip I spent a couple of weeks in McLeod Ganj, the home of the Dalai Lama in the foothills of the Himalayas near Dharamsala. I heard from an Englishwoman, who lived way up in the mountains, about two young Sai Baba devotees who possessed ash and objects that they believed had been materialized by the saint. Unfortunately, I could not go with her because there were too many people in the car. A few days later, while taking a taxi to her place to hear about her visit, I discovered the driver was a Sai Baba devotee who had taken many tourists to the homes of these young devotees. I booked him for the next day and invited three other Western wanderers to go with me.

Driving to the town of Kangra, about an hour from McLeod Ganj, we passed through beautiful farmland. Perhaps the lower altitude made the crops grow better there than around Dharamsala. As we drove, I recalled Mick Brown's book, *The Spiritual Tourist*, in which he tells of visiting homes of Sai Baba devotees in London and seeing the ash on pictures and objects. On one hand, I thought how wonderful it would be if ash started appearing in my house. On the other hand, how would I explain the phenomenon to the ordinary Western visitor who is skeptical of anything non-scientific?

The driver took us directly to the home of Grisa, a young woman who lived in New Kangra with her parents. Her father worked in Shimla and returned only on weekends. Their two-story house, large by Indian standards, featured a garden with grass and flowers. Grisa and her mother welcomed us and shared their story. Some eight years earlier Grisa began seeing the form of Sai Baba, which was not visible to other people. According to Grisa and accounts in books, Sai Baba appears to devotees in body. Even her parents could not see him when he appeared to her. Then, she explained, he sent her written messages. She showed us a black, ringed notebook filled with pages of notes, mostly in Hindi, that had appeared to her spontaneously. She said they were messages of encouragement for her spiritual life.

Grisa and her mother gave us water and juice before taking us upstairs to a room devoted to Sai Baba, where there were a few pictures of the great man. The ash did not cover his big hair, as was the case in Mysore, but seemed randomly distributed over the pictures. On the floor were lines of red ash that had appeared a couple of months earlier. Grisa had one small object that Sai Baba had materialized for her recently—a blue stone about two inches long, called a *Shiva lingam.*

A *lingam*, associated with the male phallus or creative power, most commonly sits upon an oval base called a *yoni*, the name for the female organ, and is worshiped by followers of Shiva, a Hindu deity. By this time, I was used to seeing the faithful pour coconut milk over *lingams* or place marigolds around them, but I remembered my astonishment the first time I saw this type of worship. Shiva represents pure power, both creative and destructive. It's not surprising that Hinduism, the most biological of all religions (think hatha or physical yoga), associates the sexual processes with its most powerful deity. I say "deity" because there are many Hindu deities and sometimes thousands of forms of one. But even a beggar on the street, if asked how many gods there are, would reply, "One."

While we Westerners find this ambiguity difficult to understand, Hindus are perfectly comfortable with the representation of God in many aspects. Still, many devote themselves to just one or two aspects of the greater God. Didi, for instance, worshipped Hanuman, the monkey god of the *Ramayana* who represents selfless service—the ideal to which she has devoted her life.

Grisa's room did not have an abundance of ash and had just the one *lingam*, which did not sit on a *yoni*. It was just a beautiful, elliptical blue stone laying on the bureau. She said if we really wanted to see materialized objects, we should go to a house down the road in the city of Old Kangra, where a teenage boy had been inundated with materialized objects. She called to be sure he was home and went with us to direct the way, although I suspect our driver knew where to go.

We drove out of the suburban area into the old section of town. The boy, whose name I did not get, lived in a much smaller house with no garden. Even in these crowded conditions, the family set aside one room for Sai Baba. What a room it was! There was a female statue that grew hair and a rock that dripped honey. The walls were covered with pictures of gods and saints, including Jesus, and all had ash, mostly white but also red and blue, on their surfaces.

In one corner were twelve Shiva lingams, all four inches in diameter. Each sat on a yoni. The boy's experience was unique because of the abundance of lingams, not because they actually materialized. Sai Baba created them regularly. The phenomenon is, perhaps, beginning to be recognized outside of India. At the McLeod Ganj guesthouse where I stayed, I met a woman who'd come to India to investigate spontaneously appearing rocks — lingams — for a doctoral thesis at an Australian university.

When we first arrived at the boy's house, a man had come to retrieve a message from Sai Baba. He'd asked a question through the boy. The message, which pleased him very much, appeared on a piece of paper accompanied by a rudraksha seed, commonly used in India to make prayer malas, which are similar to rosaries. Although I would have liked to spend more time looking at the objects in the room, the boy had to leave to attend a school activity. Because no one else was home, we also had to leave. I tried to give him a 100-rupee note to support his work. "No money," he said. "Baba says, 'No money.'" His response is consistent with what others report, including Howard Murphet, the Australian biographer of Sai Baba.

We went back to Grisa's house where she served us tea and cookies and gave each of us a picture of Sai Baba and a book about him. She also gave me a packet of ash. We tried to pay for these gifts, but she would take nothing. We asked her if she intended to marry. (If she did, her parents would have been trying to make a match because she was in her mid-twenties.) She said, "No, I have Baba in my heart. I do not want to make room there for a husband."

Sai Baba's teachings follow the principles found in the ancient literature of India. The fundamental paradigm presented in the Vedas and the Upanishads is that of *samsara*, the wheel of existence, where the divine soul, *atman,* wanders through numerous births and deaths until it is liberated and realizes its oneness with the universal spirit, *Brahman*. Each individual is a drop in the ocean, and peace and bliss can be found only by realizing he is one with the ocean. Unfortunately, knowing intellectually that *atman* equals *Brahman* is not enough; one must realize this truth in the depths of one's being. The realization is accomplished by a variety of paths generally referred to as *yoga*, meaning "yoke," the joining of an individual soul with the godhead.

Most gurus I saw had some kind of extraordinary power, but each of them seemed to be more human than divine. Sai Baba functioned on an entirely different level; he appeared to be one who had merged with the ocean, *Brahman*, and took physical form to lead the rest of us along the path. He often stated he did not wish to be worshipped as the guru: he wanted each of us to find our own guru within.

His miracles have been recorded in hundreds of books and articles. He has materialized bowls, candy, jewelry, crosses (especially for Christians), and predictably, *Shiva lingams*. One came out of his mouth every year for Shivratri, the celebration honoring Shiva.

Indians who do not follow Sai Baba sometimes question his motives for materializing objects and accuse him of being a mere magician. I think Sai Baba wanted to show that the material world is insignificant because it can be manipulated and changed. But what cannot be changed is true reality, the *atman*, the Christ, the love, within each of us. In Volume VI of his writings Sai Baba made this assertion:

> *This Prema (love) is My distinctive mark; not the creation of material objects or of health and happiness. You might consider what you call "miracles" as the most direct sign of Divinity; but, the Prema that welcomes you all, that blesses all, that makes Me rush to the presence of the seekers, the suffering and the distressed in distant lands, or wherever they are, that is the real sign! It is that which declares that I am Sai Baba.*

Observing the materializations required a shift in my belief structure. Even though I did not become one of the millions of devotees of Sai Baba, seeing the ash come out of his hand and nectar seep out of the rock changed me profoundly. It showed me that the physical world does not have to follow the rules of science and prepared me for a deeper spiritual search.

CHAPTER 6

My Buddhist Period
and a Surprise

The trip to India influenced me in several ways. I saw that meditation can alter a person, that matter can be manipulated, and that peace, although elusive, is possible. I still longed for a group or teacher with whom my spirit could resonate and for a man with whom my heart could join. I kept hearing the bromide, "When the student is ready, the teacher appears," so I continued my spiritual search. I assumed the same idea applied to a man, though I had less of an idea about what to do in that arena. Earlier, I'd been convinced my extra pounds kept men away, but no satisfactory man appeared even as the Indian parasites I retained for more than three years melted away those pounds.

The summer after I went to India, I took two courses in religion—one on Christianity and Eastern Thought and another on Buddhism. In those courses I began reading the texts of the Eastern religions, including the *Bhagavad Gita* and the *Tao Te Ching,* as well as selected writings from the Buddha.

The *Gita* helped clarify my approach to finding my own spiritual path. It features the god Krishna, an incarnation of the preserver god Vishnu, one aspect of the Hindu trinity that also includes Brahman, the creator, and Shiva, the destroyer. Serving as the charioteer for the warrior Arjuna, Krishna gives lessons to the reluctant fighter, who agonizes over his role of battling part of his family for control of the kingdom. If he went into battle, he would perhaps kill his uncles and former teacher. Krishna instructs Arjuna about his proper role: Arjuna belongs to the warrior caste. Therefore, Krishna reminds him, it is his *dharma,* or sacred duty, to act—to fight—but with detachment.

Later in the *Gita,* Krishna tells his student there are four paths to God, paths applicable to people of all religions. Arjuna's is one of *karma,* meaning action or work. Arjuna, therefore, should dedicate his work to God and do his duty through the action of battle. In the twentieth century, Mother Teresa, who fed the poor and cared for the dying in the streets of Calcutta, serves as the star example of karma yoga in the modern world. One weekend of feeding homeless people, who happened to be unappreciative, gave me new admiration for Mother Teresa and convinced me that *karma yoga* was not my path.

The most common spiritual path is that of *bhakti*, meaning worship, devotion, or love. The love of God, or an aspect of God, leads to union with God. Some Christians might worship Jesus, others Mary; Muslims, Allah; numerous Hindus, their individual guru or deity. Through love of and devotion to a deity, devotees surrender their individual desires and merge with the divine.

Many Buddhists, especially those of the Zen school, follow the *raja* path of meditation in which thoughts, feelings, memories, desires, and attachments come up from the unconscious mind and are released. The letting go frees the practitioner of these earthly bonds.

The final spiritual path defined in the *Gita* is *jnana*, or knowledge of the self, which often begins with studying books but moves into wisdom. People on this path know they have attained wisdom when they realize their oneness with God. Ramana Maharshi, a famous guru from South India, throws out a challenge to *jnana* types, "Ask constantly, 'Who am I?'"

Whether through service, love, meditation, or study, these paths or disciplines lead to the same end, merging the individual *atman* with the universal *Brahman*. Or, as Krishna says, "Whoever knows me without delusion as the supreme spirit of man knows all there is, Arjuna — he devotes his whole being to me."

The *Gita* helped me understand that I predominantly followed the *jnana* path, although, like most people, I could see part of myself in each of Krishna's four disciplines. I had been attracted to studying literature because the great writers deal with the big questions of life. I liked going to therapy to study myself, and I liked observing the gurus with their extraordinary powers. Knowing that *jnana* was my way made me understand why I did not become a devotee of Sai Baba and why I could not, even as a child, worship Jesus, and why I felt inclined to proceed with study.

At the same time, the course in Buddhism made me think maybe I could become a Buddhist: perhaps I already was one without knowing it. To eliminate suffering, the primary aim of Buddhism, certainly appealed to me, as did the Buddhist teaching of rebirth. There is no permanent self in Buddhist doctrine, so what is reborn is not an individual soul but the karma collected from this or past lifetimes. When all karma is extinguished, there is emptiness, or nirvana—heaven, if you will. The historical Buddha, sometimes called The Enlightened One, transcended ordinary reality and entered into a transcendent state. All but the Buddhist idea of "no-self" fit with the beliefs of my father and grandmother. Daddy could not bear the thought that there might not be an individual soul.

Buddhism qualifies as a missionary religion. Like Christianity and Islam, it encourages converts, as opposed to Hinduism and Judaism into which a believer is generally born. From the outside point of view, Buddhism also seemed to be freer of the cultural trimmings that pervade Hinduism.

I found plenty of cultural trimmings in both Zen and Tibetan Buddhism, though. I went to a Zen center in upstate New York for an introduction to Zen Buddhism and sitting meditation. The main building, located near a lake that looked inviting to my swimmer's eye, had a large gong in front. The architecture, with its long lines, seemed Japanese—plain yet elegant.

One resident showed me my room—a tiny monk's compartment with a single bed, a bare desk, and a small picture of a flower on the wall. I wanted to chat with the resident, but this was not a chatting place. He did tell me, when pressed, that he started coming there several years ago and gradually increased his time until he moved in permanently. I wanted to ask, "What made you decide that?" but his manner told me he had given enough information. I wanted to know if the decision to move to the Zen center had solved his problems in living. I was still desperate to solve mine.

But what problems did I have, really? I had a good job, successful children, friends, and even improved relations with my parents. But I was lonely. There still was a place in me that couldn't be filled with family, friends, or fortune. Had I found a husband or lover, would my search for God have been less urgent? I felt the angst of the underlying dilemma of existence: *Why are we here? Why do we have to suffer so much?* I remember walking with a friend at the Jersey Shore, enjoying the feel of the damp sand on my wet feet. A seagull flew down and pecked at the sand, searching for some juicy morsel. "Is that what our lives are like?" I questioned, pointing to the gull. "Is our purpose only like his, to get as much—money, possessions, or even prestige—as we can?"

"Why do you bother with questions like that?" she responded. "It is such a waste of energy." I felt chastised and realized many of my friends did not share my interest in exploring unanswerable questions about life.

For years I had embraced materialistic goals, determined to overcome the poverty of my childhood. My former husband and I pursued success in school and work. We had staked out the territory and plowed through the tasks. My father's view of reincarnation and retribution started looking materialistic to me: do good things in this life to get a good next incarnation. As a child, I found reincarnation a happy alternative to the hell those Sunday school ministers raved about. But, as an adult, I wasn't so sure. Another life might just be more hell. Even my search smelled of spiritual materialism. I was checking off religions if they didn't feel just right.

The Indian trip and the courses in Eastern thought helped me integrate the Hindu-Buddhist view that the purpose of life is to realize one's true nature and be liberated from *samsara,* the cycle of death and rebirth. The goal was self-realization, enlightenment. Buddhists speak of the wheel of existence from which we all must ultimately step. I hoped sitting meditation would provide a path to that goal of enlightenment, though I was rather sure I would not achieve such a sublime state in this lifetime.

The resident showed me the Zendo with its two long rows of mats down each side of the room. He gave me a brown cotton wraparound robe, told me the schedule for meditation and meals, and left me to return to my room. I wished I had a roommate because I felt forlorn. I also felt constrained by the sheer number of rules. I couldn't help berating myself for coming. I had to remind myself: *You want a spiritual discipline. You can't find that by reading books. You have to have the experience.*

The thought of the next day presented another worry: *Would I be able to sit through the meditations?* I have never been able to sit cross-legged, much less in the lotus position, so during the meditation periods, called *Zazen*, I sat on a cushion with my legs tucked under me. That first morning I survived the chanting, done in the Zendo, and two 35-minute meditation periods with a five-minute walking meditation between the sessions.

By the time it was all over, my head was pounding from caffeine deprivation. I hurried off to my room, took off my robe, and realized I didn't know the protocol for getting to breakfast. I assumed there was a protocol. Sure enough, a resident came to get me, told me to put on my robe, and took me to the silent breakfast where, thank goodness, coffee was available.

For the meditation sessions we sat in two very straight lines with our eyes half open. At least that is what we were supposed to do; I closed mine in a small act of defiance. We coordinated counting with our breath—one on the inhale, two on the exhale, from one to ten. Then we started over. At first I zoned out and found myself not counting at all or arriving at 15 or even 45, but as I became more practiced in a couple of days, I stayed on my numbers. During the last session I did not lose the numbers once.

I found ways to unintentionally get myself into trouble, though. The *roshi*, or head, of this Zen center had gone to New York City for the week and left the management to a few permanent residents, who I began to think of as "the Nazis." Each time I broke a rule, someone spoke to me sharply. I made too much noise managing my chopsticks at one breakfast, and I breathed too loudly in one meditation. One infraction, occurring at the end of a long sit, landed me in a Catch-22 situation.

The procedure for walking between sessions, and for leaving the Zendo, followed a strict procedure: we had to get up, put our cushions in their proper place at the front of the mat, and fall into line to walk, not unlike soldiers marching in a parade. I was not as youthful or practiced in sitting as most persons there. In this particular meditation, my knees stiffened, requiring me to take extra time getting up. By the time I arrived on my feet, everyone was in line, ready to march out. I had to make a quick decision: *Do I leave my cushion in the wrong place or be out of line in the exit?* Thinking no one would know or care about one cushion three feet out of place, I left it there. How wrong I was. The infraction was announced at dinner.

I could have managed all that because I really liked the meditation, particularly the satisfaction of controlling my mind, if only by counting. It was the cultural things that made me know Zen was not for me. Each morning we chanted in Japanese. We ate with chopsticks, and our robes were the type worn in Japan. But what sent me fleeing—it's always the little things—had to do with cleaning.

Everyone at the Zendo had to do some work, with the residents overseeing the visitors. I was assigned to kitchen cleanup. A blonde, attractive woman nicknamed Himmler—I didn't make that up—ran that show. The tasks included washing the cabinets and appliances and cleaning the large cement floor. Before she abruptly left, she assigned each of the kitchen crew a task: I was to mop the floor. I looked every place for the mop, but I couldn't find one. When Himmler came back to check on us, I asked her, "Where do you keep the mop?"

"We don't own one. You have to wash the floor on your hands and knees," she told me. "That is the way they do it in Japan."

Something in me revolted. Getting down on my hands and knees reminded me too much of weeding onions. Every summer of my high school years Lynette and I had crawled along the rows in Oregon, clutching a small triangle tool we used to remove weeds that grew close to the delicate onion plants. We felt lucky to have work and make a little money for school clothes and our one-night vacation, but at this point in my life I didn't have to make money or get anyone's approval by laboring on my knees. I just would not do it. A couple from Ohio, longtime Zen sitters, didn't seem to mind, so they did the work without me.

I decided to leave. I told the resident in charge I was leaving because I had come especially to be with the *roshi*, whom I had met previously, and that I couldn't fulfill my mission because he wasn't there. What I really wanted to escape was the cultural overlay epitomized by the way they cleaned the floor. Perhaps I could have embraced an American Zen, but at that time none was well known.

I discovered the Tibetan Buddhist Learning Center in Washington, New Jersey, not far from where I lived. It held Sunday services. I took some classes there and twice heard the Dalai Lama speak (before he became an international celebrity). The learning center owns a large tract of land with several buildings, including a temple, a teaching center with a kitchen, a large room for classes, and small, bare rooms for students not unlike those at the Zen center. There is also a house for the husband and wife who manage the place. Wildflowers and meadows grace the landscape, and most summers the walkway to the teaching center is lined with multicolored zinnias.

The temple where we went for prayers or ceremonies featured brightly colored decorations, inside and out, and looked like many I'd seen in pictures. The main room, large enough for two hundred people, usually had no furniture because most people sat on the floor, though chairs were available. Along the front wall was a row of big golden Buddhas fronted by pictures of the Dalai

Lama, small statues, and offerings of all sorts. The offerings, whose purpose I never fully understood, sometimes changed from week to week, but often were bouquets of flowers, both fresh and artificial, containers of water, packages of cookies, cans of evaporated milk, jars of fruit including maraschino cherries and mandarin oranges, candy, and money. Once, there was a container of pennies, another time a twenty-dollar bill.

At each end of the altar were shelves of books—not regular books but packages of wooden slats with scriptures and commentary written in Tibetan. The slats, wrapped together in brightly colored satin, some with brocade at the ends, contained the ancient teachings and commentary of Buddhism. The shelves were built higher than the three largest statues to show that the teachings hold more importance than the persons. The center's founder, Geshe Ngawang Wangyal, a Kalmyk-Mongolian guru, brought some of the holy writings to America in 1955. Others came later.

In the early days, the classes often would be given by a Tibetan monk and translated by the American caretaker and teacher who had been at the center almost since the beginning. He had learned to speak and read Tibetan, both ancient and modern, from the late founder. One weekend, many of the original students of the founder had returned. We were listening to a teaching when someone in the audience questioned the accuracy of the translation. Soon a discussion or debate broke out in Tibetan. Half the students took part. *How incredible*, I thought, *all these students can speak Tibetan.*

Tibetan Buddhism has produced many enlightened persons, so it had some attraction for me. If, however, I had to spend years learning Tibetan, I could very well grow old and die before I even became a serious student. I continued with classes though, still searching for that elusive spiritual path.

In one class, I learned a culture-free meditation technique. The leader asked us to focus for a minute or two on a person for whom we had strong positive feelings, then a person for whom we had strong negative feelings, and finally a person for whom we felt neutral, such as whoever pumps the gas at a neighborhood station. We were to picture these three persons in our minds until we felt the same about all three. That technique has stayed in my repertoire to this day, especially when I find myself disliking someone, particularly a powerful political figure.

The founder had encouraged his students to go to graduate school and get doctorates in Buddhist studies. In another class just for women, led by one student who had earned such a doctorate, the talk was more personal. Many participants had been born Jewish, some Christian, and they spoke of the difficulties of changing religions. One former Christian told of dreaming of a Buddha on the cross. She understood the image of a crucified Buddha, signaling a new stage in her movement from Christianity to Buddhism. Like her, I wanted to be a Buddhist, but my next experience took me back toward Christianity, or at least toward Jesus.

My children kept spending summers with their father, giving me freedom to do things that interested me. In an attempt to have something in common with my father and to continue my search, I took a weeklong class at the Association of Research and Enlightenment, Edgar Cayce's nonprofit center in Virginia Beach. My father always wanted to see the buildings he'd read about, to walk the ground Cayce had trodden, but I did it for him.

The content of the week, "Discovering Your Soul's Purpose," has become a blur. Not one of the many lectures stayed with me, but one guided meditation remains clear. We met in a room in the "new" building and sat in comfortable chairs, not crossed legged, much to my relief. The leader asked us to close our eyes and concentrate on our breathing. I'd had enough experience meditating by that time that I could quickly drop my thoughts and concerns about the physical world. She took some time getting everyone settled and then asked us to take a walk to a place we found pleasant and closely observe what it was like. I saw myself going to a steep riverbank with some rocks and a few windblown pines. The air was pure there and the water gurgled below me. In my mind's eye, I sat halfway down, near the rocks.

She asked us to picture a friend with us. My friend, whose face I never saw, wore a long white robe and had long, brown hair. A feeling of recognition came over me. *My god*, I thought, *it's Jesus. But I don't want Jesus; I want Buddha.* I tried, without success, to push the picture out of my mind.

The leader's voice continued, "Bring an animal into the scene." My annoyance intensified when a little white lamb appeared. I recalled the ministers in the Sunday school of my childhood talking about the Lamb of God, something I'd never quite understood. I wanted to resist Jesus and the lamb, but I seemed trapped either by the leader's voice or my own vision.

"What object is important?" the leader intoned. A staff appeared in Jesus's hand.

By this time I was no longer aware of the leader's voice. She may have given the instruction that our friend should say something because mine did. He turned away from me and walked up the bank, away from the river, with that little lamb beside him. He waved the staff over his head and said, "Follow me." *The nerve! How could I follow him? I gave up Christianity when I was a teenager, just about the time Grandma left, and hadn't had any inclination to take it up again. How could Jesus just come into my mind like that?*

I did not tell anyone of this experience for more than a year. Finally, I told a friend, a psychotherapist.

"It is part of you," she said. "It can't be ignored." But I did ignore it for more than five years. I returned to the Tibetan Buddhist Maitreya Festival, held every year in August to honor the coming Buddha, called Maitreya. A large statue of him, along with other Buddhas, sits in the temple. (The idea that there are many Buddhas and all of us are on our way to Buddhahood particularly appealed to me.)

Lots of people attended the festival; I recognized some of the students from former classes. Monks marched in red robes. They carried flags and performed rituals. Most people, including me, had no idea of the meaning of the flags or any of the rituals. I stayed awhile and visited acquaintances. But because I couldn't connect in a meaningful way with the events, I became bored and left before the festivities ended. As much as the Buddha and the ideas of Buddhism appealed to me, I saw no way of being a Buddhist. The cultural divide, as with the Indian guru system, seemed too difficult to cross.

One day that fall Ravi burst into my college office unannounced, his face glowing with inner light. From a bag that he carried, he pulled out three books, all part of *A Course in Miracles — Text, Workbook for Students*, and *Manual for Teachers*. (They since were published as one book.) Often I'd heard mention of the course, and someone at the Edgar Cayce workshop had spoken highly of it, but I had no idea where it came from or what it was about. I didn't know at that time that these books contained a philosophy that would solve my life-long conflicts between Eastern thought and Christianity, Buddha and Jesus, my father and mother.

"I thought you would like it because it is about miracles," Ravi said. "I couldn't relate to it. It sounds too much like the Bible for me."

What a miracle it turned out to be for me.

CHAPTER 7

Finally, a Man

Just before my last child went off to college, I began to worry about what I'd do with myself without having a child to look after and bring meaning to my life. As with that first night my former husband moved out, the problem wasn't how I would occupy my time but how I would cover up the emptiness that still gaped like a hole inside me. If I shifted even one rock in my defensive position, that hole could open up like a crevasse in a glacier and swallow me.

My former husband and I had learned duplicate bridge in graduate school. We'd even earned a few master points before children and careers dominated our lives. I decided to play again, but finding a bridge partner looked impossible, especially since I didn't even know the location of a bridge club.

At that time, in the mid-1980s, the newspapers had just started running personal columns so I combined my needs and ran an ad for a partner for bridge and "possibly other things." Several men and one woman sent answers via the mail. I responded to only one.

On my first date with Charlie we discovered our common political stance, love of reading, and interest in spirituality, but mostly I saw Paul Newman blue eyes. It wasn't love at first sight, though his jaunty look in a gray chapeau appealed to me. He was twenty years older, but one would never know it by looking at his muscular body and cute, rounded butt. We each had three children, an older boy and two girls, and our girls had almost identical names.

We played bridge with a group of his friends, and although he had a logical mind, it became obvious to me he'd never move beyond a basic bridge level. He didn't have years of card games flowing through his veins as I did. By the time I concluded I didn't have a duplicate bridge partner, though, I found I had an excellent life partner. His wife had died twenty years earlier, requiring him to raise his second daughter on his own. He was just moving from an engineering career into retire-

Charlie and me in 1990.

ment and wanted to partner up before he spent much time at home.

Charlie voraciously read and consequently knew a lot, but he didn't have to let everyone know it. He also listened. His daughters had trained him: "Don't try to solve my problems. Just listen to me talk about them."

He also gardened, growing shrubs and flowers. At his place he had cotoneasters that produced red seeds in the fall on the side of the house as well as yellow coreopsis moonbeams mixed with purple Russian sage in back. The same red tulips bloomed every year in front of the house, but what I liked best were the clematis vines that climbed over the brown fence that separated his yard from that of his neighbors. One plant produced dark purple flowers, but the other sported blue blossoms. They weren't the heavenly blue of my grandmother's morning glories, but appeared just as vibrant because they were set against the dull fence, and they comforted me in the same way.

A couple of years before I met Charlie, I found out why the morning glories were so significant to me. In another attempt to get over my emotional difficulties, I consulted a therapist in New York City who used the Rubenfeld Synergy Method, developed by Ilana Rubenfeld. The method integrates bodywork and psychotherapy. The therapist had me lie on a massage table. She aligned my body in a precise way and then lightly touched various parts of my body as we talked. I was not even talking about Grandma when she put her hand on the soft spot just below my sternum. Suddenly, the image of blue morning glories came to mind and the floodgates opened. I cried for fifteen minutes, longer than I had cried over anything in my life, as I blubbered over and over, "Grandma, why did you leave?"

After I stopped, the therapist and I spoke briefly about my feelings of abandonment. Then she had me get up from the table and look at myself in the mirror.

"Look at your face," she said. "Do you see how bright and alive it is? Think of the energy you have spent holding that grief." Although the experience was a great relief, my fear of abandonment didn't vanish with that one session.

About a year after we'd been dating, Charlie asked me to go with him to Boston to visit his daughter and her fiancé, Pat, who were considering buying a house. They wanted Charlie to look at it structurally with his engineer's eye. We arrived late in the afternoon, checked into our bed-and-breakfast, and met the young couple to go see the house. I almost felt as if I were part of this family.

They were buying the house from the owners, not through a Realtor. Something the owners had said to Pat made him think they didn't want many people coming into the house. "I don't want a lot of people messing up this deal," Pat said, "so if it would be OK with you, Myrna, I would like you to wait in the car."

The words shot from his mouth to my heart, moving a defensive rock, and the crack opened up. I could say nothing. Charlie said, "Myrna will be fine." But I wasn't fine. Typical of me, I kept the pain to myself.

The three of them went into the house while I cried, first while sitting in the back seat. Then I got out of the car and walked around, saying to myself, *You've got to pull yourself together. You can't let them see you like this.*

My mind darted to other times when I had cried uncontrollably. Once a dean at the college where I taught criticized a report I had written. Much to my horror I burst into a flood of tears, unable to explain myself. Then there was the time a professor on my dissertation committee told me I had to write another chapter in my doctoral thesis. Again I cried as if I were falling into some endless void with no solid place to get my footing.

Where had it all begun? Maybe at home when I felt left out whenever I saw Daddy and Lynette talking, as they frequently did. I didn't want to tell Daddy anything about my life or feelings, but I wanted his attention. I remember one incident when I was about twelve and Lynette was fourteen. We were to help Daddy seed the large field near the Sunday school in clover. We each had a broadcaster, a bag for the seed with a handle on the side that turned a metal fan on the bottom. The hole in the bottom of the bag could be opened to let the tiny clover seeds fall on the fan, and as we turned the handle, the seeds flew out two or three feet in all directions. The three of us started out together, but as we went along, I could not keep up. Lynette had such long legs and stamina that she kept the pace with Daddy.

I suffered because I was so much more competitive than she was. I wanted to be the best in everything. Yet I was falling farther and farther behind. Worse yet, I could see them talking to each other.

Within an hour Daddy and Lynette were striding along at one end of the field and I was trudging along the other end, tired of carrying the bag of seed and turning the handle, but mostly tired of being left out.

That is the way I felt in Boston—left out when I wanted to belong. My over-the-top reactions to all these small events gave me glimpses into that dark place in my psyche that I preferred to leave undisturbed. Maybe Pat's comment hit the bull's-eye on the abandonment issues I felt when my grandmother and Gary left. But maybe I took every opportunity to feel victimized by those who proclaimed to love me. What was I to do with this familiar feeling of the ground giving way beneath me? By the time the three of them returned, a half hour later, I had the tears stanched but not the ache in my chest.

We went to an Italian restaurant where the three of them ordered starters and wine in addition to their main course. They were in a celebratory mood. I ordered only veal francese, one of my favorite dishes, and ate very little. Twice during the meal when they started talking about the house, I felt tears welling up so I excused myself, went to the ladies' room, and cried. Even at the time, my behavior reminded me of a silly soap opera. Why would anyone have such a reaction to such a tiny event? On each trip to the bathroom I waited until I stopped crying and washed my eyes with cold water to dim the redness. I was away from the table more than I was at it. Finally, we left.

When Charlie and I got into his BMW and started driving, his first words burst out with anger, "What in the hell is wrong with you?" That opened the floodgates of tears again, and his tone changed from anger to sympathy.

"Tell me what's bothering you," he said.

"I feel so left out," I wailed. "Just like I did with my family. Daddy and Lynette always talked, but they never included me."

We went back to our bed-and-breakfast. Charlie knew I had trouble sleeping in strange beds and hadn't yet found comfort in sleeping with him, so he had reserved a room with twin beds. We lay on one of the tiny beds while he comforted me.

"You can talk about this all night if you want," he said. I knew talking wouldn't do it. I felt so broken and longed to feel whole, so I stroked him, first on the bottom and then in front. As he entered me, the pain subsided. With each wave of orgasm, it drifted away like the outgoing tide.

A few months later I moved in with Charlie, and we settled into a companionable life. He had one flaw—overly angry reactions to even a small deviation from his expectations. Once, before we lived together, we had agreed to buy a Christmas tree for my house and then go out to dinner. I had some time on my hands so I bought a tree by myself, thinking that we'd have more time for dinner. When I told him on the phone, he accused me of not keeping my agreements, hung up, and didn't call me for a few days. When he called, he said something about punishing himself even as he had tried to punish me.

After we moved in together, he would have one of these upsets every six months or so. I had no idea how to respond to them; maybe fear of his leaving me made me unable to properly defend myself. For about five minutes he'd carry on and then not talk for two or three days. When the emotional storm had passed, he returned to his loving self. I would have objected more to his outbursts if I hadn't been so happy. I felt as ecstatic then as when I sat in front of the morning glories watching the lightning with my grandmother, as blissful as during the first five years of my marriage. But his outbursts did keep me on guard. After he got sick, five years into the relationship, we were in the car when he began one of his angry attacks. I slowed down enough to look at him.

"Stop it now," I said. "I will not tolerate this ridiculous anger." He stopped. Unfortunately, I'd had to wait until he was in a weakened condition before I could stand up to him.

Although we continued to play bridge, even at the local duplicate club, Charlie only advanced to the intermediate level. Our most enjoyable card game was cribbage, a game that I'd played with my grandmother. It has brought me so much comfort and joy that I taught it to my children and grand-children. Especially after one of Charlie's angry spells, cribbage would bring us back together. We kept a running score for who won the most games, one moving ahead for a while before the other whizzed by. Often a cribbage game would lead to the bedroom where Charlie exuded love through every cell, and that love seeped into my naked skin and filled me with contentment.

Although my spiritual longing ebbed, it did not subside, and came to the fore whenever Charlie and I fought. I began reading the books Ravi had given me, *A Course in Miracles*, but I couldn't grasp their meaning. Ravi was right. It sounded a lot like the Bible. It was written from the point of view of Jesus and referenced passages in the Bible, but with different meanings. The *Course*, for example, holds that Jesus's statement, "No man cometh unto the Father but by me" doesn't mean he is in any way separate or different from us except in time and that time doesn't really exist. Also, The Last Judgment becomes "a final healing rather than a meting out of punishment." These statements all make perfect sense to me now, but then they just confused me.

One word that appears many times in the first few chapters of the *Course* is atonement. At that time I was attending a Quaker Meeting—a good place to meditate—so I asked parishioners there how they understood the concept of atonement. One person said, "To become one with, as with God." A helpful definition. I liked what little I understood of the *Course*. I had not, however, read past chapter four and had not even opened the other two books, *Workbook for Students* and *Manual for Teachers*.

At times I felt "at-one-ment" with Charlie, a state that replaced any spiritual urgency. We took several big trips out west together, but I liked the simple things — taking walks or watching birds. We went to Atlantic City to the bird sanctuary, to Cape May to check out the birds and ride the ferry to Delaware, to the Delaware Water Gap to climb the mountain that overlooks the Gap.

One winter day we went hawk watching by driving up and down the major highways where the heavy traffic creates just enough warmth to attract raptors. As usual, we saw a few red-tailed hawks, a Cooper's hawk, and a couple of types we couldn't identify. Charlie always had such enthusiasm for any bird-watching activity, but we hadn't been driving long that day when he said he needed to go home and rest. Soon after, he began losing weight. He went for a colonoscopy. Polyps were found and one was cancerous, but it seemed to be contained. A few months later, a chest x-ray revealed a spot on Charlie's lung. He had an operation to remove part of the lung, but some cancer cells had grown into the lining of his chest cavity.

He went to the cancer ward of the local hospital for his first treatment. It was quiet there compared to the medical-surgical floor. We talked for a couple of hours while waiting for the chemotherapy. It was the last pleasant time we enjoyed until three days before he died. Chemo made him nauseous, weak, and bad tempered. Although he never stayed in bed, life revolved around his treatments and his sickness. We tried to talk about his dying but found it easier to live in denial. Some time earlier, when death looked far off, we both had said we couldn't understand why people hated to think of their dear ones dying alone because that was what both of us wanted. Dying seemed too personal to have someone watching.

One morning when I woke up, Charlie was dressed in his khaki pants and long sleeved shirt even though it was the end of July. He even had on his chapeau.

"I am going to the hospital," he said. "Do you want to take me or shall I call the ambulance?"

We drank a cup of coffee. Then I drove him to the emergency room, stopping to buy a newspaper on the way. He received relatively rapid attention, only having time to glance over the sports page and finding that Barry Bonds had not gotten a hit. He asked the doctor who examined him if he were a baseball fan. When the doctor nodded, Charlie said, "Barry Bonds has been hitting so poorly that he should sweep the stadium to earn his salary." The doctor and I chuckled.

Later that day, after admitting him, the doctors determined there was nothing more they could do. During the next three days his daughters both came to see him. His son was too bereft to make the trip. Charlie wasn't listed as critical, but I had seen him turn away from life and told the son he was dying.

The son, who was a physician, asked me, "What do the doctors say?" The doctors' main communication had been with the older daughter.

"I don't know what they are saying," I responded, "but I know what I see."

The daughters and I agreed we would leave Charlie alone for twelve hours to give him a chance to die if he wanted. So we said good-bye around five in the evening. He got out of bed about four in the morning to sit in the chair, according to the nurse, who put him back in bed and made him agree he wouldn't get up again. He died two hours later.

One of the sympathy cards I received had a note attached suggesting persons in mourning should continue to talk to the departed person. My conversations centered on one topic — the house — because Charlie's handiwork was everywhere. On the original house Charlie had done the finishing work himself and later added a sun porch. He installed the hardwood floors and, at sixty-eight years old, put on a new roof. Also, Charlie had kept a clean house. He liked order, an attitude that encouraged me to be neater than I ordinarily am. After he died, I let stacks of paper pile up. I didn't attend to those hardwood floors. I started feeling bad about the way I kept the house, so I began speaking to him to assuage my guilt. Sometimes I spoke the words out loud: "I can't keep this house picked up, Charlie" or "Look at this pile of papers. You wouldn't have tolerated that" and "Sorry, Charlie, I just can't keep these floors looking the way you did." These conversations made me feel as if he were still there.

Three months after he died, I asked Maude, a psychic friend of mine, to come over to determine whether some subtle form of Charlie—a ghost, if you will—inhabited the house. She and I belonged to a ladies' social group. At our gatherings she often would use a Ouija board to answer questions. I knew she had abilities because once she told another member of the group not to worry because her house would sell soon for a specific number. She was two thousand dollars off, but it was a six-hundred-fifty-thousand-dollar house, so who's quibbling? Maude also had been asked more than once to communicate with ghosts that inhabited old houses. One of her "ghost busting" activities had been written up in the local newspaper.

She entered, sat down on the couch in the sun porch for ten minutes, and said, "He is not here, but let's see if the Ouija board has anything to say." We sat at the kitchen table. Though we both put a hand on the board, Maude controlled the rapid movement from one letter to the next. I wrote them down in a row with my free hand. The first line — "Do not connect the house with me" — took my breath away. He had been listening to me!

The next line — "I left so show" — was incomplete. The third line should relieve me of any fear of dying — "The transition here was so easy, really easy." Then he said, "We were good for each other. Now you must grow strong, but you won't be alone. Love Char." How true the message, "you won't be alone," turned out to be, as I discovered ten years later while working with a mystic.

When the clematis bloomed that first spring, they reminded me of my losses. The following year, I moved out just as they began blooming. That time they reminded me of the love and support I still had, not from the physical presence of my grandmother, Gary, or Charlie, but from the love I had experienced, especially from Charlie. It was a love I could keep alive in my heart to nourish me in the next stage of my journey.

CHAPTER 8

A Course in Miracles

ithin a month of Charlie's death, I once again began looking for a way to fill the void, which was more manageable than after Gary had left. Instead of looking for a church I began attending two classes at the New York Open Center in Manhattan—one in hatha yoga and one in *A Course in Miracles*. Neither satisfied me, but both set me on paths I continue to this day.

The teacher of the class for *A Course in Miracles*, a dynamic woman, made it sound wonderful and soothing by using familiar words: "forgiveness," "Jesus," "God," "Holy Spirit," and, of course, "atonement." Not entirely reconciled with Jesus, I asked if we had to believe in Jesus to accept the precepts of the *Course*. She assured me we didn't. In fact, she said, that point had been a stumbling block for her when she started studying because of her Jewish background. Also, the language annoyed me. It was masculine, just as in the Bible. The teacher shared that she, too, had been bothered by the language, but the message of the *Course* had helped her let go of that concern.

One point from the *Manual for Teachers* appealed to me because it contradicted what the ministers from that little Sunday school I attended had taught—that we had to accept Jesus Christ as our personal savior or spend eternity in hell. In contrast, *A Course in Miracles* states, "This is a manual for a special curriculum, intended for teachers of a special form of the universal course. There are many thousands of other forms, all with the same outcome." The *Course* maintains its main advantage is the saving of time.

Those initial classes didn't add up to any clear understanding for me, but some part of me knew I had to pursue the *Course* further. The New York teacher had studied with Dr. Kenneth Wapnick, known as "Ken" to his students. Later I would find out he is the world's foremost authority on all aspects of *A Course in Miracles*. Better yet, his organization, The Foundation for *A Course in Miracles*, was then located in Roscoe, New York, a few hours from my home. Unfortunately for me, it moved to Temecula, California.

The following summer I was off to Roscoe. What I heard there was not comforting, but disturbing and disarming. But first to the story of the scribing of *A Course in Miracles*, a story which can be found in the beginning of all second and third editions of the *Course* and in most books about it. Helen Schucman and William "Bill" Thetford, both psychologists with doctorates, worked together in the psychology department at what was then called Columbia-Presbyterian Medical Center in New York City. Bill was chairman. I call them by their first names because I feel as if I know them from the many stories Ken told about them in his lectures and books. Although both had Jewish backgrounds, as did Ken, they didn't describe themselves as believers. Indeed Helen called herself a militant atheist.

Bill and Helen worked together successfully though they didn't get along with each other or other members of the academic community. One day in 1965, as they were preparing to go to a meeting at another university hospital, Bill made a now famous speech to Helen declaring there must be "a better way" to conduct business than to attack each other and their colleagues with academic vituperation. He thought they should be more cooperative and loving. Surprisingly, Helen agreed to help him find this better way.

The conversation triggered something in Helen, who began having vivid dreams and experiencing strange images that continued for three months before a Voice—not a sound but an inner dictation—said, "This is a course in miracles. Please take notes." Panic-stricken, she called Bill and asked what to do. He suggested she do what the Voice asked of her. So she began taking down the words in shorthand. If the Voice were interrupted, say by a phone call, it would pick up exactly where it had left off after the phone conversation. Each morning, or at lunch, Helen read to Bill what the Voice had dictated to her the previous evening, and he typed what she said. The process went on for seven years. Neither ever considered stopping. They took on the task as if it were an assignment both had agreed to complete.

Helen never doubted the Voice was that of Jesus, but she wasn't pleased about what it asked her to do. As Ken recalls in several of his books, she even resentfully asked the Voice, "Why did you choose me? Why didn't you choose a nice holy nun, or someone like that? I am the last person in the world who should be doing this."

"I don't know why you say that," the Voice replied, "because, after all, you are doing it."

The *Course*, written mostly in blank verse, comprises the 669-page *Text*, the 365-lesson *Workbook for Students*, and the 72-page *Manual for Teachers*. Later, two pamphlets—*The Song of Prayer* and *Psy-*

chotherapy: Purpose, Process and Practice—came through Helen. When Bill and Helen finished the original project, the Voice said, "Amen."

But they had no idea what to do with the material. Enter Kenneth Wapnick, who holds a doctorate in psychology and who at that point in his life had converted to Christianity. Ken's intention was to go to Israel and then enter the Trappist monastery to which Thomas Merton had belonged. A priest-psychologist who was a mutual friend of Ken, Bill, and Helen, had asked Ken to look at the material Helen had taken down. When he read it, Ken knew immediately that the material spoke a profound truth and that he wanted to spend his life working on it. As he has said many times in books and classes, the *Course* is the best integration of psychology and spirituality he has ever seen. He worked with Helen to divide the texts into chapters, to insert headings, and to make minor edits, such as taking out material directed personally to Helen and Bill. Otherwise, it stands as Helen transcribed it.

The *Course* was popularized by Marianne Williamson and Gerald G. Jampolsky in *Return to Love* and *Love is Letting Go of Fear*, their respective books. Since then many books have been written about *A Course in Miracles*. Those first books, though, present such a sweet version of forgiveness that whoever read them would naturally be attracted to the *Course*. But neither one states straightforwardly what forgiveness means, which was one of my difficult lessons when studying that first summer with Ken. I remember going over the steps of forgiveness with a fellow student: First, recognize that the problem is in me, not with the other person. Second, acknowledge that the problem inside me is one that I made up. Third, ask the Holy Spirit to take the guilt away. That didn't make sense to either of us because the *Course*'s concept of forgiveness depends upon at least a partial acceptance of the metaphysics of *A Course in Miracles*, something I had not integrated into my understanding.

Neither Williamson nor Jampolsky say directly that, according to the *Course*, the world does not exist. But a central idea of the *Course* is that the world — indeed the entire universe — is not real: it is an individual and common projection of the one Son of God, that one Son being all of us, Jesus included. The Buddhists teach that the world emerged from karma, and the Hindus assert the world is *maya*, illusion, so the idea was not new to me. Studying Christian Science and seeing the Sai Baba miracles contributed to my accepting the *Course*'s assertion. In fact, I found relief in the idea that God did not create the world. Even as a young person, I could not reconcile an omnipotent, loving God with a God who would create this kill-or-be-killed world with its disease, poverty, premature death, and endless wars.

According to the *Course,* the only true reality is Oneness, Heaven. We, the one Son of God called the Christ, seemingly did the impossible and separated from God. I say impossible because the *Course* says that the separation never really happened and that we are merely dreaming of exile from God. Then, another split occurred in the mind of Christ — right-mindedness and wrong-mindedness. Right-mindedness encompasses such things as forgiveness, atonement, and holy relationships while wrong mindedness is identified with the ego and its fellow travelers — sin, guilt, fear, and special relationships. So even though the *Course* states "there is no world," it doesn't ask its students to deny their experience, but rather to re-interpret it.

The *Course* depends heavily upon the idea of the unconscious mind, that iceberg of repressed guilt that lives in us, according to Sigmund Freud. We act in a way that we call sin. Because we fear punishment, we repress the memory of the action. According to Freudian thought, anything repressed must be projected onto the world. If a child steals an apple from the supermarket, for example, he fears punishment, so he denies his action, represses his guilt, and then projects that guilt. He can project it outward by being angry at an authority figure or inward by getting a stomachache.

Although we are unaware of it, our greatest suffering comes from the guilt of having separated from God. Because we feared God's punishment, the *Course* explains, we created the world. Actually, we projected the world and continue to project it from our common ego mind in order to hide from God and avoid his punishment. The idea of eternal hell comes from this fear. The most original idea in the *Course,* found in neither Hinduism nor Buddhism, is stated in the *Workbook for Students*: "The world was created as an attack on God."

In the book of Genesis, God observes after each day of creation that "it was good." This view could not be further from the point of view of the *Course,* which calls all material creation a *"mis*creation." God created only his one Son, made in "the image and likeness" of Himself and who is therefore spirit, which is eternal. According to the Introduction, the *Course* is summarized in these three sentences: "Nothing real can be threatened. Nothing unreal exists. Herein lies the peace of God."

Although the creation stories differ between the Bible and *A Course in Miracles*, the idea of man's fall serves as an appropriate metaphor for humankind's separation from God. Because Adam and Eve disobeyed God by eating the apple, humankind suffers. In Genesis, God metes out the punishment: putting enmity between men and women, causing women great pain in childbirth, making women dependent upon men—a real horror—and making men bring forth thistles and thorns from cursed ground. No wonder we needed a place to hide from God! According to the *Course*, we provide our own punishment because we feel so guilty.

Because we are creating the world with our projections, to create peace, and ultimately heaven, we have to withdraw our projections. When we see only love, we are only love. So if a boss insults a worker and the worker's feelings are hurt, the worker must metaphorically "turn the other cheek," or in *Course* terms, withdraw his projection of hurt or anger and ask the Holy Spirit, Jesus, or the universe (if one is an atheist) to help see the situation differently. As Jampolsky writes, "People have to give up the idea that someone did something to them because no one has the power to take the peace of God away from anyone."

I didn't want to accept that idea because I had built my life story around being a victim. "How can I not be a victim?" I asked Ken. "My grandmother left me when I was thirteen. My husband moved across the country and left me with three kids, and my partner just died."

Ken, who never wavered from the principles of the *Course*, said, "You have an abandonment script." I later understood that I was trying to heal from my guilt, perhaps that fundamental guilt of believing I had abandoned God. As for Grandma, Gary, and Charlie, they were just playing their roles. No one comes into this life without a script written in concert with those with whom we entered. I needed to forgive myself for choosing to feel abandoned.

The idea is that nothing actually happens to us that our minds don't create, so we must forgive ourselves for having hateful, angry, abandonment, or even killer thoughts in our minds. Another person, no matter who it is, is merely the deliverer of the message of our own minds. So we must forgive him for what he didn't do. I had to forgive Grandma, Gary, and Charlie in order to forgive myself for creating abandonment in my life. Ordinarily, we forgive people for what they did do. But that interpretation puts two people at different levels: the forgiver would be saying he is such a good person that he will let go of the lesser person's transgressions. The *Song of Prayer* pamphlet calls this "forgiveness to destroy."

Forgiveness brings a shift in perception and seeing the world differently *is* the miracle.

Even if one cannot completely accept the metaphysics of the *Course* – Helen Schucman, the scribe, thought only five or six people would accept it – its method for eroding the ego and identifying more strongly with God, Christ, Allah, or the Right Mind can be helpful to anyone. We are to look at our own sin, guilt, or fear, acknowledge we are responsible for our perceptions of any situation, and turn all of it over to some higher power. We should not, however, judge ourselves for our feelings of sin, guilt, and fear. Judging one's errors creates more guilt, which again will be repressed into the unconscious and again projected outward or inward. These projections create illness, aggression, anger, difficult relationships, and ultimately war.

After two introductory classes, I made a big commitment and signed up for a series that met one weekend a month for four months on the topic "Projection Makes Perception."

In my mind I accepted what the *Course* taught as truth, but that doesn't mean I could integrate that truth into my life. I had been annoyed all my life by my parents' eating habits: they both made noises when they chewed because they had ill-fitting false teeth. My mother's teeth clicked through every meal. My father avoided the clicking by chewing with his mouth open, producing a chomping sound. Then that annoyance spread to my father's chewing gum, then to Gary's chewing gum, then to anyone chewing gum or chomping food. I had talked about this endlessly in therapy, but nothing had helped, so I asked Ken about it in one class, exaggerating my parents' offenses to match the disgust I felt. It took quite a bit of nerve to do this in front of a class because I felt a lot of shame about being disgusted by my own parents, but something in me desperately wanted to heal.

In a loving voice, Ken said, "The world will agree with you that you are justified in being offended. But remember we will go to extremes 'to keep the face of innocence,' and that is what you are trying to do. As long as your parents are the offending ones, it is not your fault." He was right. In telling those therapists, who had to be on my side, I could keep the disgust glued right to my parents instead of bringing it back to my own mind. But Ken did not give me an inch of wiggle room. He made me realize part of me wanted to hang on to my own life story, the story of victimization.

Ken, or perhaps an advanced student, pointed me to Lesson 132, which states, "The world is nothing in itself. Your mind must give it meaning. And what you behold upon it are your wishes, acted out so you can look on them and think them real. Perhaps you think you did not make the world, but came unwillingly to what was made already, hardly waiting for your thoughts to give it meaning. Yet in truth you found exactly what you looked for when you came."

So I wanted those clicking teeth and chomping jaws. But for what?

A line in the next paragraph gives hope for perceiving a different world: "Change but your mind on what you want to see, and all the world must change accordingly. Ideas leave not their source."

So what was my way out of this disgust? To forgive myself, of course. First, I had to acknowledge the shame. Then I had to recognize that the self-hatred was in me. Maybe I projected my self-hatred onto their mouths because both kisses (affection) and praise come from mouths, and those were two things I wanted most from my parents, Gary, and Charlie.

Each class gave me hope that I could escape the psychic pain of my life, so I signed up for another long course, this one on special relationships, one of the big ideas in the *Course*. Oddly, because it is such an important concept, the idea of special relationships does not come up until the second half of the text. Special relationships come in two forms — special hate and special love. Special hate presents no difficulty. We project onto someone else things in ourselves that we cannot tolerate and then hate that person for them. We avoid looking at our own guilt by projecting it onto them, as I did with my parents.

Special love, however, is not so simple, even though it follows the same pattern, namely, projecting our guilt onto someone else. Ken explained the "scarcity principle": we, in a separated state, feel incomplete and unfulfilled. As the *Course* points out, God is what's missing. When we choose God, the ego is undone. But instead of turning to God, the ego side of our minds constantly looks for ways of feeling whole through special relationships, usually by falling in love, but also through food, alcohol, drugs, work, sports, money, shopping, or other activities and obsessions. When I was young, whenever I felt bad about myself and that vague emptiness moved up into my chest, I tried to fill the spot by overeating, a problem those parasites solved on that first trip to India.

Most commonly, we fall in love with someone who has qualities we lack and therefore admire. That person can satisfy our special needs. If that person also falls in love because we have something they lack, the world thinks we have an ideal relationship. Actually, the opposite is true because we don't have love. Instead, we have dependence. As long as one keeps satisfying the special needs of the other, and vice versa, everything is OK. But when one stops, difficulty starts.

Finally, I saw how this dynamic worked in my life with men. One of the major things I desperately wanted from those around me was recognition. Early on I learned I wasn't going to get it by being beautiful or having a great body, but I saw I could get it by being good in school. Because my parents didn't seem to value my achievements, I gave up on seeking recognition from them. Gary, also smart and a high achiever, entered my life just after Grandma moved. We encouraged and praised each other for our good work in school. Everything went swimmingly through six years of dating and five years of marriage, at which time an irrevocable change occurred. I became pregnant.

I completed my master's degree in June. By that time, Gary was working night and day on the research for his doctoral dissertation in animal nutrition. That summer and fall I no longer had to read books and write papers for my own class work, so I often went to the lab with him and even carried out some of the simpler tests on various machines. I became very large in that pregnancy, my belly almost touching the spectrophotometer, or whatever machine I operated.

Our son was born right when Gary had about a month's more writing to do. The delivery had not been easy so I didn't feel right. I failed at nursing and didn't sleep well. I had to sit on a donut as I helped with the drawings for the dissertation. The pressures of Gary's dissertation and his job search overshadowed the joy of having a baby.

I'll never forget the day Gary brought his dissertation home, all typed out and fastened in one of those black binders. In the acknowledgments where students thank their dissertation advisor, the school, anyone who contributed to the research, and finally their wives and family, he thanked me first. Logic tells me I should have been thrilled: he had recognized my contribution. He showed it to me, took me in his arms, and kissed me. I felt nothing. He was getting the doctorate. I was a mother.

I understand now that my bad feelings about myself, what the *Course* calls guilt, could no longer be contained. He couldn't give me enough recognition for having a baby and for helping him with his dissertation, and I certainly couldn't give it to myself. He received all kinds of recognition for his doctorate, including a new job. My intelligence meant nothing. We stayed married another thirteen years, had two more children, and even experienced some periods of love, but mostly we were unable to satisfy each other's great needs. Because we didn't know how to talk about them, our special love turned into special hate: I could blame him for everything wrong in my life, and he could blame me for what was wrong in his.

A Course in Miracles says that special love is an unconscious form of special hate because we are dependent upon the specially loved object, and being dependent reminds us how incomplete we are. To change a special relationship into a holy relationship, we must, of course, forgive that person for everything they did — actually did not do — to us. As we forgive, we release our own guilt and so have less and less to project onto the other person. As we have less need to receive recognition, phone calls, and sweet talk from that special person, the relationship transforms. In a holy relationship there is no this-for-that. There are no bargains. Those in a holy relationship do not say, "If you call me four times a day, I'll make you dinner. If you buy me diamonds, I'll give you sex."

At one of the classes a man about fifty years old asked, "Is it all right if I tell my beloved that she is beautiful, or is that making it a special relationship?"

"It depends," Ken answered. "If you see her as beautiful and want to express your love, what could be better? But if you expect something in return, the compliment turns into a bargain, and that is special love."

I stopped going to Roscoe five years before the foundation moved to California. I'm not sure why. Maybe I thought I understood the *Course* well enough to read it on my own. It is designed for self-study. In addition, I began attending a Unity church that emphasized *Course* principles. When examined honestly, though, I see I stopped because once I left those introductory classes, I encountered more serious students who, between classes, stayed in their rooms and listened to Ken's tapes. They didn't want to go for walks or swims or engage in long personal talks. I liked the social aspect of those early classes. When that didn't exist to the degree I wanted, I was less willing to make the effort to go. In truth, I wasn't ready to confront any more of my own issues.

Once, when Ken returned to speak on the East Coast, I went to hear him. His depth of understanding of the *Course,* combined with his compassion for every person in the audience, made me realize how much I could learn from him. I had the urge to move out to California so I could attend classes regularly, something I could have done for five years when the foundation was still in New York

State. But I, the student, hadn't been ready, even though the teacher had appeared.

CHAPTER 9

Guidance from a Mystic

inding a path to God and finding God are two different things. Once I had begun studying *A Course in Miracles* I never doubted that it was my path or that it was the truth. Somehow I thought that because my doubts about beliefs disappeared, the problems with my life would follow suit. My body showed me otherwise.

I had herniated a disc four months after Charlie's death. I treated it with physical therapy, acupuncture, exercise, and finally microsurgery, mitigating much of the pain. Two years later, after I had moved back to the house on four acres, I worked hard one day moving ten-foot poles from a fence to a stack on the other side of the lawn. When I woke up the next morning, I wasn't able to stand for more than a minute or two. I had herniated the same disc again. I repeated many of the treatment options I'd done before, this time even going to New York City to see Dr. John Sarno, the author of *Mind over Back Pain* and *Healing Back Pain: The Mind-Body Connection*. Having read *Mind over Back Pain* before I went to see him, I knew he would tell me my symptoms were related to difficulties with my emotions.

He asked me to lie on a massage table. Then he poked several areas on my back, shoulders, and buttocks and declared my symptoms to be Tension Myositis Syndrome, or TMS, brought on by repressed anger. "Not just anger, but rage," he proclaimed. Sarno theorizes that pain is an unconscious distraction from deep emotional issues. When patients recognize that their back pain (or gastrointestinal disorders, migraine headaches, or skin problems) are only a distraction, their symptoms serve no purpose and go away.

I didn't disagree, though I felt no anger. Going to his lectures and reading his book multiple times did me absolutely no good, although I realize his recommendations work for many people. So I had a second operation, which got me out of the six-teen-ibuprofen-a-day pain regimen and made it possible for me to continue working. Long after the operation, my lower back and leg still felt weak and mildly painful.

The parasites I'd picked up in India and carried around for three years apparently had weakened my digestive system. Alternatively, the repressed anger that Dr. Sarno said he detected was express-ing itself in my intestines. Every year or so I'd get an attack of diarrhea that would last a month or two, sometimes longer. I saw several specialists, but nothing physical seemed to be wrong with my digestive system. One gastroenterologist told me, "You should consider changing your life." I couldn't have agreed more, but I didn't know what to change.

In desperation, my younger daughter, who lives and works in New York, took me to China-town to a health practitioner, Ms. Li, who'd been recommended. The window outside the shops ad-vertised "healthful herbs," "ginseng," and "relieve pain cream." We found Ms. Li in a tiny store on Bayard Street that sold scarves and tee shirts as well as Chinese medicine.

"Is Ms. Li here?" my daughter asked. "I heard she practices Chinese medicine."

"Yes, I am Ms. Li. Come into the back." We followed her to a very small room with just two chairs; my daughter had to stand. Ms. Li took my wrist and felt my pulse. I knew from my acupuncture treatments that Chinese doctors use six pulses in the wrists to diagnose illnesses. "Mother very weak. Too much fire." She then took my pulse again and, addressing my daughter, repeated, "Mother very weak. You must take care of Mother. You cook good food for her."

We walked back to the store where Ms. Li bagged up sticks and bark that I was to boil in water for an hour. She instructed me to drink the resulting herbal tea, one of the worst tasting concoctions I've ever ingested. She told me to return, but the thought of another round of that drink discouraged me from following that course of action.

I concluded from all my attempts at relief that my mind, albeit unconsciously, held some guilt, anger, or rage I hadn't yet released, but I felt at such a dead end. I didn't want to go back to psychotherapy because that would require rehashing the stories of my life about my parents, grandmother, and former husband. Going to another round of medical doctors also didn't seem to be a good solution, especially because two had conjectured my back pain and diarrhea probably had to do with my mind. About that time my older daughter — thank goodness for children — heard of a woman, living not far from me, who did some unusual healing work.

April Moon lived in the country in an old, clapboard farmhouse with two main rooms on the first floor, a dining room and a living room. A small bathroom and a small kitchen, which extended from opposite sides of the dining room, had been added to the original house. In the living room, which doubled as an office, I sat on a comfortable chair beside a table that held religious figurines and bottles, writing paper, and a pen. On one wall was a large collage of the Buddha and, on another, a small icon-like painting of the Madonna. Three other paintings hung on the walls. Yet somehow the room felt stark.

April, a woman in her fifties, looked elegant with her long blonde hair, makeup, and a long dress she wore loose to cover up some extra pounds. We chatted for a while, and then I told her ever so briefly about my health problems, especially the long bouts of diarrhea. She waved her pen, saying, "That's enough."

Pen in hand, she sat and waited, listening and apparently no longer paying attention to me. Then she wrote. She stopped, listened again, and wrote. Although she doesn't explain her methods in detail, she says she works under the guidance of the archangels. In matters of health she hears from what she calls the "Team of Healers," which are "forces of nature" that unite when "the soul and the Divine Lights come together to heal." When she works with emotional issues, she listens to the client's "Higher Self," which knows the entity's purpose in this life but which does not have the ability to heal. She told me once that she doesn't actually hear words. Rather, she feels energy that she has to interpret. Sometimes I heard her whisper, "Do I have that word right?" or "Should I read that to her?" or "Should I revise that sentence?"

In that first session the Team of Healers said, "Whole milk needs to be started immediately. Take three cups a day—morning, afternoon, and evening. Eat the following foods—grains: rice, oats, corn, buckwheat. Eliminate gluten foods such as wheat, rye. Add veal, milk-fed quality, four ounces every other day for three weeks. No other meat during three weeks." I was astounded by the specificity of the instructions.

At this point she must have heard something about supplements because she got up to retrieve a catalog from her shelf and then continued listening. I was to take "CellMins Multi-Mineral Without Iron, two morning/two evening" and a vitamin supplement called "Radical Fighters, one morning/one evening." April does not sell these supplements; she sells nothing but her time and talent.

Her instructions continued, seemingly contradicting the advice about avoiding gluten foods: I should eat "barley, cooked to be very soft and fluid, with onions and mushrooms each day between 5:00 p.m. and 7:00 p.m. for three weeks. Two tablespoons of barley in two cups of water cooked for one hour with onions and mushrooms." The rationale: "The barley water will help regulate the spasms of the intestines by clearing them."

Lo and behold, in three weeks I was over that round of diarrhea. When it has recurred, I eat barley gruel.

Along with those very specific instructions about food, the Team of Healers also gave general advice. I should read the works of Helen M. Luke, a writer of books about psychological interpretations of literature and about aging. "Money will take on a different meaning," the forces said, "if you spend time reading Helen Luke."

I had said nothing to April about money, but the trouble I'd had with poverty as a younger person persisted. Evidently, the spirits—probably some part of myself—perceived that my anxieties over money contributed to my health problems. I read the books. I am unsure whether they helped, but money issues no longer live in the forefront of my mind.

How ironic, I thought after the initial session. I had criticized my father for investing so much energy in Edgar Cayce and his readings. Yet what I just experienced didn't differ significantly from a Cayce reading, except that April does not go into a trance to receive information. Also, someone, usually Cayce's wife or secretary, recorded his readings and kept copies that have been typed, sorted, and made available for anyone to use. In contrast, April writes out her readings herself and gives each of her clients the one and only copy. There will never be a collection of April's work and so no way for someone else to benefit from the readings. Perhaps that's a good thing. Ken Wapnick often pointed out, "The curriculum (suffering and any treatment) is individualized." Appropriate guidance for one might not be efficacious for another. Eating almonds, as Cayce had recommended for shrinking the tumors of one man, did not cure all cancers, my father's included.

Six weeks after that first appointment, I went to April about my back problem. The Team of Healers gave me advice about taking my supplements: "Back limited improvement with low mineral uptake. When taking minerals, do so thirty minutes after drinking milk. This will allow the intestines to be prepared to take up the minerals. With the addition of the milk, minerals, and the CellMins, the deficiency can be addressed and slow down the desorption. Calcium release from the milk form is better than any other form." *Is that true just for me?* I wondered. I'd read many modern books about healthful eating that recommended cutting out all dairy foods.

After a year of taking the Radical Fighters and CellMins, another reading said I should stop both and switch to a simple multivitamin and a mineral supplement. The Team of Healers also told me to take Choline Cocktail, an energy drink, to help remove from my system the heavy metals I'd assimilated in India.

One day, the Team of Healers recommended that I eat rice twice a week, and then gave advice about wheat and rice that might be beneficial for a larger audience: "Wheat is not an inborn habit; it is a substitute. Throughout humankind's history it has substituted for what could not be obtained. This is not the case with rice. Rice is nutritionally in balance with the foods that build, not sustain. Across this country an imbalance in nutrition is occurring from the daily use of wheat. Rice, on the other hand, will give you the nutrition you need to balance the other foods you are eating. Rice is not given as a substitute for wheat but as a balancer for the food you eat."

The next month the Team of Healers recommended I see a chiropractor for adjustments to the neck to "aid in opening the spine to more flow of energy." I was to go two times a week for six weeks. Next, I was to begin an exercise program to strengthen the muscles of my back, arms, and shoulders. This included doing yoga and lifting weights. They also said I should eat watercress and spinach, and drink carrot juice.

Along with the specific instructions to improve my health came explanations of spiritual matters. My Higher Self said in the same session about strengthening my back, "You grasp too tightly to the past, Myrna. You need to love what you are now and stop loving what you were. Your spirit is strong, your will does not want to accept the weakening of the body, yet you have the strength of spirit that comes *only* with the weakening of the body. See the truth of this and rejoice." I could not rejoice. Although I wanted spiritual strength, I disliked that I had to pay in declining physical strength. After all, I was barely sixty.

In one reading, April connected my back problems with my competitive nature, which has been integral to my psyche since first grade when I decided to be the head of the class. My Higher Self said, "Is it possible to express yourself without wanting to be better than someone else? Everything you do is done with a competitive flare. It is a mindset that tightens up your back and throws it out of alignment. It is a mindset that has its origin in your mother's low self-esteem. As a child you fought with her about needing more than she had to give. You decided then that you were going to be a winner. Any time you feel you have not won, you tighten your back so you can feel the physical pain and not the anguish of defeat."

One evening, when my back felt particularly painful, I received a phone call from April. She said the Team of Healers had notified her that I needed some relief. She told me to recline on my bed and receive healing energy she would send. Five minutes later, as I lay on my bed, sensations—pleasant, tingling feelings—moved up and down my spine. They lasted five or ten minutes, after which my back pain, though not cured, was alleviated.

When the pain recurred, the Team of Healers recommended I see one of April's other clients, Dr. Eleanor, a chiropractor. Eleanor practiced what is called "network chiropractics." Doctors trained in this method work with several patients at one time, lightly touching one patient in certain places on the back and neck before moving to the next one. A few minutes pass before the chiropractor returns to any one patient. Sometimes she applies pressure; other times she touches the front of the body. The physical contact is always gentle. April and I went together to see Dr. Eleanor, April for her knee and me for my back. The trip to Dr. Eleanor's office took two hours.

After that, the Team of Healers told me to find a network chiropractor nearby. I did and continued to see him every week for more than a year. *Why didn't they tell me that originally?* I wondered. It made me think that perhaps sometimes April must know something before she can interpret the messages she receives.

Often advice about the physical and the psychological came together. Once, the Team of Healers said, "Your body takes a beating every time you lose your focus on yourself and put it on managing others." As a teacher and single parent, managing others seemed natural to me. By the time of this reading, however, my children had left home, and the average age of my students was about twenty-eight. Nobody needed managing.

One reading from my Higher Self addressed my problem of loneliness: "Fear of being alone has been with you since you were a child feeling left out. Your reaction to feeling left out has been to function in a constant state of engaging others. Engaging others is what humans must do to know they exist. That is not the issue. The issue is the constancy of it for you at the exclusion of time engaging your inner self." April then wrote that the next few sessions would be about bringing self and others into balance "as the anxious bowels and fearful back are all symptoms of this imbalance."

Sometimes the Team of Healers would announce they were going to work on specific issues, but by the time the next session came around, they addressed something else. Perhaps I had something more pressing to work on, or they, like humans, forgot what they were thinking about. A third possibility is that they continued to work on the issue and I just didn't recognize that they were.

One particularly disturbing reading addressed what I perceived as leftover shame about my childhood poverty and my attempts at overcoming what I interpreted as the narrow lives of my parents. I was told, "You don't think so, but how others see you and how to make connections is always on your mind. There would be no considerations of shame otherwise. Your mother was so unconnected socially that all you can ever think about is social connectivity." That was true. Mother never had coffee or tea with neighbors and didn't go to parties, just to church. The reading stated that Mother "was not clever in social situations." According to the Team of Healers, my response was to be clever in order to make myself feel connected to others. Unfortunately, the preoccupation came at the expense of connecting with myself, which was precisely what I needed to do to improve my health.

One reading directly stated that the conflicted nature of my mind actually strained my back. Like Ravi, I wanted to live in the world. I kept up a social life and played competitive bridge, even going to tournaments around the country, and also carried on with my career. Also like Ravi, another part of me wanted to live the spiritual life. The Team of Healers addressed this conflict: "This has created a strain on the spine that has continued since 1983 until recently."

The trip to India in 1983 must have intensified the conflict because it deepened my spiritual connection. After that trip though, I'd made no changes in my exterior life.

"Moving the spine with manipulation has helped relieve the strain," the Team of Healers said. "Yet it can also become a source of resistance if you do not change with it. Your spine does not know how to move; it receives mixed messages. While this is a common dilemma among humans, it is in you because the two messages are diametrically opposite. Because of the severity of the extremes, you have suffered without breaking from either."

My body gave me messages, and April interpreted them. But could I hear them well enough to change my life? The last fall I taught I could not stand up all day because of the weakness in my back. The readings recommended that I take a semester off and then retire.

I'm not sure when my lower back, where the herniations had occurred, got better, but one day I stepped sharply off the curb onto the street. For the first time in years I felt no pain or weakness. I even skied after that, something I hadn't had nerve enough to do when my back felt so weak. What caused the strengthening? Was it working with April and releasing some thought patterns? Releasing the rage? Taking those high-powered supplements? Seeing the chiropractor? Stopping work? Doing yoga? They'd all occurred over such a long period of time that I couldn't attribute healing to any one of them. I only know that the Team of Healers, speaking through April, had been the director of the process.

Once my health improved, April channeled instructions from my Higher Self to make my life more satisfactory and spiritual. Her words often came with a directness I tolerated because I always could see truth in them. In an early reading my

Higher Self said, "You are a spiritual butterfly just as you have been a social butterfly." I couldn't deny that, but as the message proceeded, it became more damning:

Now is the opportunity to settle into a slower pace and achieve the harmony you have sought here and there. You have been a social butterfly to promote yourself and now the hold it has on you becomes your way of seeking spirit. To be alone without others to take note of you is almost unbearable.

Promoting yourself and protecting your image is why you are unable to be alone. Who are you without all this activity? When you dig into this question you will finally let go of all the partying and die to it. As long as you promote this self-image you cannot be alone. The horror of what you suspect you are is a driving force for this promotion and partying. Work and play have become the vehicles for it.

As difficult as it was to hear, the entire message was true. I recalled sitting on the green couch the night after Gary had moved out. The loneliness had been almost unbearable and I didn't want to experience it ever again. Though I had lived alone, except for the few years I lived with Charlie, I had filled my life with a social network of friends, bridge, and work so that I could ignore the poverty of my own soul. But that day I was called out.

What was this horror I suspected I was? Maybe, as Freud would say, I was sitting on an iceberg of unconscious self-hatred and guilt. When I decided I probably was, I no longer found the thought so horrifying. Maybe if I would just forgive myself, as *A Course in Miracles* recommends, I could, over time, find my own company more pleasing.

CHAPTER 10

Talking to the Dead

*a*pril also transmitted messages from the dead. Had these messages not referred to specific events, I might doubt their truthfulness. But who could doubt when she told me things I hadn't told anyone? One day in the middle of a session, she announced a spirit had entered. Immediately she gave herself a few drops from the bottle on her table, a flower essence, and wrote, "This spirit has 'trailed' Myrna since Aug. '92," the month Charlie died. I immediately thought of the promise that had come through on the Ouija board: "You will never be alone." I wish I could say I felt his presence, but I didn't.

The summer he died we'd had a conversation at the kitchen table about his care and my younger daughter's hefty college tuition. Charlie was frail from the ravages of cancer and chemotherapy. Though we both knew he was dying, part of us lived in happy denial. I told him that if I were to stay home and care for him, he would have to contribute to the tuition bill. Otherwise, I'd have to teach two courses in summer session. I left the decision up to him. He chose the latter so I was gone much of the month preceding his death.

Ten years later, and through a mystic, Charlie gave his rationale for his decision. "What you feared about my loyalty was unfounded," he said. "My loyalty was to you and no one else — not extended to your children. Having made my choice, I was understanding of the lack of care that resulted." Couples counseling long after the event! *A Course in Miracles* teaches that time is one of our grand illusions, so what does it matter when doubts diminish and guilt goes?

I had an opportunity to go further back in time when my grandmother "came in" a couple of years later. Whenever a spirit tries to speak through April, she blocks it unless one of the archangels, usually Raphael, approves the communication. When Grandma spoke, April asked me to leave so she could confirm the communication was legitimate.

I returned a couple of days later to find Grandma still on the line. During this session I had a chance to release any negative feelings toward her and learn that the Team of Healers might include souls who have been with us in our journey toward God. Or because we are all One, her voice may have been a part of myself:

As you know, I was a presence in your life that made you into a voice of Hope. My end of presence on Earth did not end my presence in your life. I have remained a constant presence in your psyche, one that gave balance to your struggle with spirituality versus materialism. It is this struggle that causes the stomach and intestines to become ill when the balance tips towards money and therefore materialism. It has been my presence that has kept some attention on spirituality and a non-materialistic life. Without this you would have been limited to what money brings. Today I am to be a part of the Team of Healers to give you clarity on how to keep the balance or how to leave the materialistic life once and for all.

Then Grandma mentioned a psychotherapy session I'd had about her, "The session to work through your anger with my leaving threw that balance once again toward the materialistic as it weakened my connection with you."

How could I doubt these comforting messages came from Charlie and Grandma? They both referred to events about which no one knew. Their speaking so specifically added fuel to the view that there is no place to go—no eternal heaven or hell. Our lives and afterlives are just a journey. In his "Thought for the Day," Sai Baba writes:

> *Life is a long pilgrimage along the rough and tortuous road of this world. This journey does not have any halts; it is one continuous journey, through tears and smiles, through birth and death. When the road ends, and the Goal is attained, the pilgrim finds that he has traveled only from himself to himself, that the sought was all the while in him, around him, with him, and beside him! He himself was always Divine.*

The importance of belief, the basis for my parents' quiet war, receded further in my mind. Charlie had been an active Eastern Rite Catholic, but he attended church for the reason my mother did—to connect with his roots. On the other hand, Grandma had embraced no specific religion and looked for truth where she could find it. Both Grandma and Charlie had stayed with me, not because we shared a religious belief, but because we shared love, the universal teaching in all religions.

April told me she has the ability to receive communication from a dead person for about a week postmortem, sometimes longer. My younger sister Davida, who had been working in Haiti, first as a teacher and then as a Christian volunteer at an orphanage, died unexpectedly in the fall of 2003.

The death certificate lists the cause of death as pneumonia, but in Haiti no one seems to investigate seriously. Living on the East Coast, I assumed the responsibilities for our family. I made arrangements with people in Haiti about the cremation of her body and a service. I also made reservations to attend with my younger daughter, who speaks French fluently. Before we went to Haiti though, I visited April. Davida's message to me can be understood only in the context of her life, a life filled with trouble and torment.

Although never diagnosed, she had all the signs of someone on the autism spectrum and probably had Asperger's Syndrome. Mainly, she was unable to decipher the emotional content of any face or conversation. She was smart and verbal, but could not follow a conversation if more than one other person took part. As a child, she stuttered, had no intimate school friends, and often was the victim of taunting. Like the rest of us siblings, Davida went to that dilapidated Sunday school with our mother. But unlike the rest of us, she stayed and accepted the messages of evangelical Christianity. She waited until she went to college, away from our father's judgment, before she announced that she had joined the Assemblies of God church. Even our mother was horrified and wanted none of our neighbors to find out. "They are the holy rollers," she declared. "They talk in tongues." Davida, already living on the fringes of the family because of

Davida and me in Vancouver in 1998.

her disability, moved herself further away with this decision.

Davida tried to convert all of us, but worried particularly about our father. The last summer we all gathered in Oregon, Daddy's health had deteriorated and death didn't appear to be far away. Indeed it wasn't; he died two months later. Several times Davida spoke to me about the possibility of Daddy's accepting Jesus as his personal savior. She suffered over her belief that he, a kind and loving man, would burn in hell. Mother's soul, Davida believed, could slip into heaven because she attended Christian churches all of her life. What she thought of her siblings, I can only guess.

Davida finished college and even earned a master's degree in special education. She taught elementary school but held most jobs for just one year before being asked to move on. At two Christian schools she stayed longer—nine years at the last one in the United States. But finally it, too, let her go. That's when she went to Haiti, the only place she could land a job. She lived there five years and taught the first three before she was fired. They said it directly this time—"for social incompatibility." At the orphanage she took care of children with physical and mental handicaps. She potty-trained a couple of older children, helped one to learn to take a few steps, and kept them fed and clean. She finally gained recognition and appreciation for her work.

April's message from Davida to me began, "My honor is at stake. This is what I want from you. My mother is to think of me as a missionary." Our mother resided in a nursing home and lived only two months longer than Davida, though she had lost none of her mental powers. In life Davida felt that neither parent really loved her, but even after her death she wanted recognition from the one family member she thought shared her religious views.

The message continued, "I know that whatever you think comes from your kind of mind, but it is you who can make our mother understand that my death is the end of noble work here on Earth. This is what I ask of you. Whatever else you do is of little concern to me."

The message continued about our relationship, fraught with guilt on my part because I had often become annoyed with her:

I want you to be free of any torture about us and offer you this simple truth to relieve you. If you will accept it, then I can move through this with peace. I ask that you give this to our mother before you leave for the island. I have my reason and it comes from needing her focus before I make this break.

If you will call her and share this message in your own words, then I can be at peace as I break away. Beyond this I feel honored to have been loved and cared for in my simple state by this family and the friends who have taken me under their wing as a weak one to be protected. Now I look forward to the Glory that awaits me.

I shed tears as April read the message to me. With the last line I cried not for her death but for the end of her suffering.

I called our mother and impressed on her that Davida had been working as a missionary, that she had done important work, and that her life had been dedicated to her Christian ideal. Whether I convinced her, I cannot say. Our mother had her own opinions.

When my daughter and I went to Haiti, we spent several days at the orphanage, a fenced compound. The buildings for staff were close to the entrance. The children lived at the far end of the property in dormitories surrounded by open space where the children could play. My daughter bought a soccer ball and played with the able children. We met the ten disabled children with whom Davida had worked. They lined up in their wheelchairs in the hallway of one of the dorms where they stayed all day. At mealtime a woman from the kitchen shoved food into the mouths of those who couldn't feed themselves. Some of the children who Davida had toilet trained had reverted to diapers. Davida had written out exercises for each child, but the staff had burned those instructions, along with her private papers. Was she preparing for her death?

Person after person told us Davida did noble work for which she received no regular salary, just donations from family and friends. It would be impossible, everyone said, to replace her.

In my first session with April after the Haitian trip, Davida came through once more, "Now is the time when you should lean on the Christ. I say this to you knowing you have kept yourself for another. Yet that other is no different. With this I say my final good-bye and give my appreciation of your attendance at my memorial and my mission, in hopes that you will not forget that you have a life to give as well."

What did she mean by "the Christ?" Was it the Christ of the evangelicals or the Universal Christ that exists in everyone? The middle line puzzled me, too. Was she asking me once again to believe in the crucified Jesus Christ, who would only accept believers, rather than the teacher Jesus, the elder brother of *A Course in Miracles*? I don't think so. It appeared she had softened in her belief and broadened her perspective. And what of that last line? Would I be happier and more fulfilled if I gave more of myself to others? The question remains with me to this day.

When our mother died two months later, I was with her at the nursing home in Oregon. I wondered if losing a child was just too much for her. Being far from home, I asked my older daughter to have a session with April. Mother spoke only one line, "Peace is all around me and I want for nothing." But the message contrasted with how the spirits said my mother lived her life: "Her own development set the stage for a life that was wholly focused on dealing with wanting what she did not have, but in a passive way, not an aggressive or tormented way. Yet her wanting was all inclusive and the way she worked with it was to be totally in it. To be it."

That part of the reading rang true. Mother had wanted to go to college, but after a health crisis in her second year, she never returned. Instead she married Daddy. She regretted not finishing college and spoke of it for years. She was determined her children would attend. The three daughters did, but her son received his training courtesy of the U.S. Army.

In the poverty of my youth, Mother made nutritious meals from inexpensive foods. During several long stretches she bought no meat because of the cost. She always made sure, however, that she served vegetables at lunch and dinner and had some kind of citrus fruit for breakfast through every winter.

Mother made many of our clothes and bought others at rummage sales though she made them over to look new. One winter she tore apart a worn-looking wool coat and put the nice inside wool on the outside so Lynette would have a "new" coat. Many an evening she darned socks, inserting a burned-out lightbulb in the toe or heel so she could firmly hold it as she sewed. After my father became a janitor and they had a regular income, her skillful stretching of every dollar became less critical. At that point, though, she began to recede from life. After we children left home, Mother began falling into periods of depression that became longer as she aged. She couldn't recover the meaning in life that she'd found in feeding and clothing a family on pennies. Had the want of money provided her a path to a meaningful life?

The other point that came through in April's reading indicated that Mother wanted her children to have what she did not: "To have children that wanted and were driven to reach." Were she and Daddy at odds about their children's achievements? Maybe Mother encouraged me to be at the head of the class more than I remember. Maybe she liked those ambition bumps on my head, the very ones that Daddy had ridiculed.

These messages channeled through April connected with something I'd learned from a workshop I took with the Quakers. The leader made an astonishing comment: "Have faith, not for salvation, but for revelation." I could hardly trust my ears, having attended, at an impressionable age, that Sunday school where the ministers and teachers pounded into our little hearts and minds the necessity of believing "to be saved." Believing so that I might be guided in life gave me a new perspective. *A Course in Miracles* also emphasizes that perspective. In Lesson 69, the *Course* states, "Have confidence in your Father today, and be certain that He has heard you and answered you. You may not recognize His answer yet, but you can indeed be sure that it is given you and you will yet receive it."

Certainly Grandma's message about the material versus the spiritual life and Davida's thought about leaning on the Christ felt to me like words from the divine.

I can't help but wish these messages would come to me directly rather than through a mystic. However, my "kind of mind" — to quote Davida — trained to order and analyze, probably will not suddenly open to a flood of messages from the universe.

Within a month of Mother's death, I went to my older daughter's house for coffee and a talk and to offer her Davida's leather gloves. Also visiting was a friend of hers who'd been receiving messages from dead people for as long as she can remember. In fact, she makes a living "counseling" between the living and the dead. I'd found Davida's gloves in her winter coat that I sent to Goodwill, along with other winter clothes she'd kept at my house. The gloves were too small for my daughter. The friend put them on and immediately said, "Who did these belong to?"

She began to get pictures of two women talking. She said it was Davida and our mother. "They are working things out," she said. She also reported a man wearing farmer's clothes near them. She thought he was Daddy, but "he wasn't saying anything."

Working things out, I mused to myself. Just as Daddy had implied when he returned to pay for his hat in Penney's: If you don't do it now, you have to do it later.

CHAPTER 11

Deepening Spiritual Awareness

T he Team of Healers recommended that I go on a spiritual retreat, one on which I didn't spend energy criticizing the rules. They must have known my pattern of trying out and discarding religious groups or practices because of some peripheral issue. They also must have wanted me to spend time with myself. I went to an eight-day silent retreat at a Catholic conference center led by two nuns who taught Thomas Keating's Centering Prayer, a method of silent contemplation.

Not significantly different from meditation practiced by Buddhist groups (except that we sat on chairs, not on cushions), the method came out of Keating's study of Hindu, Zen, and other Buddhist practices. A Benedictine monk, he had observed that Americans were deserting traditional Christian churches in droves and heading to meditation centers so he used a section of The Sermon on the Mount to anchor centering prayer in Biblical terms. In Matthew Chapter 6, just before The Lord's Prayer, Jesus says, "But as for you, when you pray, enter into your inner chamber and lock your door, and pray to your Father who is in secret, and your Father who sees in secret shall himself reward you openly." Keating says the "inner chamber" is one's own heart.

My sister Davida never would meditate with me because her evangelical church taught that the devil could enter into a quiet mind. Once I took her to a Quaker Meeting and she spent the entire silent hour flipping through pages in the Bible. I don't know if she read some words or if it was just the noise of the pages that she believed kept the devil away. I was pleased not all Christians shared that view.

Each day at the retreat we watched one of Keating's videotaped talks and meditated together for three hours. The nuns encouraged us not to read or write but rather to settle deeper into ourselves through the silence. I spent a lot of time wandering the countryside, finding a pond at which to sit, trying to glimpse the frogs I heard croaking, and attempting to open my heart to the joy it deserved. When I left the retreat center at the end of the eight days, I said good-bye to no one. I had made no friends, but was I friendlier to myself? Attending the retreat made me feel more kindly toward Catholicism and Christianity in general. I can't be sure whether it cracked "the crust" the Team of Healers said I had around my heart. I didn't know then that those spirits had bigger plans for me.

In August of 2005, three years after I met April, I went to her house and plopped myself down in her chair, ready to hear more about making a deeper connection with God. In the last session the Team of Healers had accused "Myrna" — I think they meant what *A Course in Miracles* calls the ego and what they referred to as the false personality — of being "such an attention getter." I can't be sure that the Team of Healers would equate the ego and false personality, and it's not as if I can check it out. That day they asked me, "What is your concept of false personality?"

"A collection of desires, fears, and irritations," I responded.

"No," the spirits said. "It is an effort to have your dreams come true. The false personality forms as one dreams. The form of it is nothing more than a vehicle to actualize dreams." They explained that these dreams "come out of a clever device set into motion by past life experiences of greed, money, power, and position." Then they come forward in early childhood as youngsters envision achieving some goal that will give them "money, power, position."

The Team of Healers then spoke of the true personality, which *A Course in Miracles* refers to as Right-Mindedness: "The true personality is the state of the Soul and gives voice to letting go of dreams and being present."

I was with them up to that point. Then came the surprise: "So the two personalities are in conflict and you are being guided to go to India to give your 'ear' to your true personality. It is a time to hear your Soul through the letting go of yours and everyone else's dreams." Of course, I was shocked. Because I had come to trust April's guidance, however, I immediately accepted the proposition that I would go to India again. *But how? And when?*

In the next session, I was told to go as soon as possible, stay for two months, and locate a place I would like to stay longer. I was further told I should come home for the holidays and then return for a long period of serious practice. I worried about making any connections in India because Ravi, who had been instrumental in both of my previous trips to India, had died seven years before I received these instructions.

Emily, my Tarot card-reading acquaintance whom I'd met through Ravi, lived in India with her guru, giving me at least one contact. Over the years, before she moved to India, she and I had seen each other occasionally, whenever she read the cards for me. During the years I spent with Charlie, I made no effort to get together with my old spiritual friends, including Emily and Ravi. Emily and I had reconnected the day of Ravi's funeral. He had died of a massive stroke at age fifty-six. He'd had a terribly high cholesterol count—more than one thousand—and hadn't taken his medicine, thinking he could control the condition with meditation.

Ravi had suffered a heart attack a few years before the stroke. I visited him in the hospital. Seeing this beautiful, vital man hooked up to intravenous tubes and dressed in hospital whites, not his elegant Punjabi suit, made my knees weak. The smell of cleaning products, generously used to hide the odor of urine, pervaded the room. We hugged perfunctorily, the years having put distance between us. A *Course in Miracles* had convinced me the body expresses the mind, so I felt I could not treat Ravi as if his heart attack were a mere glitch of an uncooperative body. Over the years I'd watched him converse with young women, emanating a sexual or spiritual magnetism. One bright Indian woman at our college would have liked to marry him. I'm sure she wasn't the only one, but he seemed hesitant to involve himself too intimately with any one woman.

We chatted about his medical condition, but I couldn't keep my real thoughts to myself. As judiciously as possible, trusting he still stood as a spiritual ally, I said, "The heart is the seat of love. You can no longer pretend you don't have problems with your affections. Something has to change in your relationships with women."

He made the enigmatic response I've heard in others who don't want to tip their hands. "Yes, I suppose I do," he said with little conviction before changing the subject.

Maybe he did change. He began living with a woman from Southeast Asia, but he always talked as if he were, or at least wanted to be, celibate. Sex wasn't his only conflict, however. Part of his heart still lived in India.

Ravi and I had taken a group to India a few years before his heart attack. In addition to the usual tourist sites, we visited his family and old friends, one of whom proposed marriage. Another friend, a leader of an untouchable village, invited us for lunch. The thirteen of us ate on the roof of a house most Indians would not consider visiting. Eating the food would have been out of the question for most members of Ravi's Brahmin caste, which is made up of the teacher-preachers said to come from the head of Brahman, the highest and supreme God of Hinduism. That day, children of the village flocked around him. They loved Ravi and he loved them. He was at his finest as he let go of his caste identity to extend love.

Ravi seemed so at home in India, but he was at home everywhere, except perhaps his own skin. He was torn by everything in his life—between India and the United States, sex and celibacy, the world and the spiritual life. He ignited those conflicts when he broke the renunciate vows of the Ananda Marga in Calcutta and married his American wife. But maybe those conflicts had always been with him.

He tried starting meditation groups and committing himself unconditionally to the spiritual life. Like me, he hadn't been able to focus his energies. One summer, before I became involved with *A Course in Miracles,* he and I traveled to New York State to visit the Sufi Order of the West and take a course in Sufism at Omega, a retreat center. Sufism, the mystical arm of Islam, appealed to us both, especially *dhiker,* the chanting of "la ilaha illa Allah," Arabic for "there is no god but God." We also learned to twirl, like the dervishes. Ravi was every bit the spiritual butterfly I was.

He helped a group of Indians establish a Hindu temple in Central New Jersey. He made two more trips to India with an artist friend. He kept in contact with friends from Ananda Marga. But the worldly life—sex and money—tugged at him. He bought a house, taught full time, and took on extra classes for extra money. I could not believe this man: he exuded unconditional love and longed to meditate, yet he spent so many hours every week talking to unenthusiastic students about accounting. I couldn't help speculating that his conflicted life contributed to his death, and wondered about my own divided life. *Did men and money also pull me into the world? Did my false personality still build dreams?*

Ravi's funeral, held in September in his own backyard, attracted many people: women who had loved him; an Ananda Marga delegation, decked out in orange; his brother with whom I had stayed in India and who now lived in this country; and a host of friends and colleagues. Ravi's body, still beautiful, lay out in the open. Many mourners, including Emily and me, walked by and ran our hands through his black, thick hair. Late in the day the Ananda Margas conducted a service in Ravi's little meditation house. After they had completely left the room, the traditional Hindu Brahmins performed the final rituals. Finally, six men carried Ravi's body off in a cardboard box for cremation. My main connection to India was lost.

As one connection went to his grave, however, another emerged. Emily told me right at Ravi's funeral that she intended to go to India the next month to stay with Babaji, her guru, in the western state of Gujarat. When I visited her a short time later, she did a Tarot card reading for me and predicted I would be connected to her guru. I didn't mind because I had been at a meeting with Babaji when he visited this country a couple of years earlier. Emily and others had made arrangements for him to give *darshan* — a blessing imparted to students by a glance from a guru — and speak at a New Age store near my house. I arrived after work with a backache, a constant in my life at that time. About forty people attended, more than the space easily could accommodate, so I slipped down to sit on the floor near a wall. When I was there for a while, I realized my back no longer hurt and didn't for a couple of hours after I left. Rightly or wrongly, I thought Babaji had extended a healing to me. There was one impediment to my visiting his ashram: he spoke no English and had to rely on translators for English-speaking devotees.

Emily went to India for a month or two, returning to fulfill her filial duty toward her elderly mother. About a year later, her mother died and she was left with no close relatives. Not a practical person, she gave away her car and most of the money her mother had left her. "I want to go empty-handed to my guru," she told me. She did keep some money from the sale of her parents' furniture. With no other encumbrances, she moved permanently to India to be with Babaji.

But there was trouble. Due to many health problems, Emily had never been able to hold down a regular job for more than a few months. Some physical conditions had been lifelong; others might be attributable to her weak back or excess weight. In most ashrams everyone has to pay at least for food. In Emily's ashram devotees could do *seva*, or service, in place of payment, but Emily became too ill to work.

Her illness, however, did not prevent her from receiving a guest, a young aspirant twenty years her junior, who, after his enlightenment, became Tapoguna Maharaj. She had met him on a previous trip, but on this one he asked her to move with him and his parents to Vrindavan, a city two hours south of Delhi. The two events, Emily's ouster from the ashram and Tapo's offer, conveniently came at the same time.

I'd received letters from Emily from time to time over the five years she'd been in India, but it was not until April and the spirits told me to go to India that I began concentrating on her situation. She and Tapo had built a house they called the Jan Jam Yogi Ashram with her parents' furniture money. It contained a small room in which I could stay. So I booked a two-month trip in the fall of 2005. I would stay with Emily and Tapoguna, hoping I could scout out where I might go on a longer trip after Christmas.

CHAPTER 12

A Return to India,

2005

*T*he Delhi Airport had been modernized since 1983, so arriving was a tepid experience compared to my first trip. Anyone meeting passengers now must pay a small fee, which keeps out taxi drivers, baggage handlers, and beggars. I missed the brightly colored turbans, the buzz of transactions about bags and transportation, and the smell of turmeric and cumin that permeate the clothes of ordinary Indians. Emily and Tapoguna

Maharaj, both looking dignified in their long white gowns and white coverings for their heads, stood just outside customs, having paid the fee to come inside.

Emily and Tapoguna

He is young, trim, and fit. She is older, heavy, and fragile. Emily had always had lots of dark curly hair, which she almost never cut, but I saw more gray than black sticking out from her headdress. Tapo's black hair flowed over his shoulders. He also had a big black beard and mustache. I felt as if I should have touched his feet with my fingers, but something in me resisted. He wasn't my guru. I did not want a guru, but couldn't help thinking about Emily's last card reading in which she saw me aligned with an Indian guru. Maybe it was Tapo. We loaded my bags into the car they had engaged—they had assumed that I would pay because certainly they did not have that kind of money—and headed south to Vrindavan.

When we arrived, we were greeted by Tapo's parents and uncle, known only as Mommy, Daddy, and Uncle. Mommy, a solid woman, perhaps in her early sixties, spoke no English. Daddy, a tall, frail man, older than Mommy, spoke a few English words and, like Uncle, understood some. The three of them lived downstairs in an unfinished brick and cement house.

We three English-speaking persons lived upstairs in three small rooms and an open space. Tapo and Emily shared the largest of the rooms. A small room with some shelves served as a hallway between their room and the corner bathroom. My six-by-ten-foot room shared a wall with the bathroom. It featured a cement slab on which I made my bed, one plastic chair, a small book container, and a fan. I kept my clothes in my suitcase and my toiletries on the windowsill. I had brought a thin air mattress, and Mommy gave me bedding, but most mornings my bones ached from their encounter with the cement. Tapo and Emily slept on the floor with just a thin mat and did not complain.

The ashram of Tapoguna Maharaj in Vrindavan, India, 2005.

To enter the bathroom, I, like Emily and Tapo, had to go through the small room. I say bathroom because we washed there, but it had no modern facilities. All the walls and floors were just gray cement. At the higher level was the hole in the floor that served as the toilet. At the lower level were a drain and a bench for hot water buckets. Every morning Uncle would bring buckets of hot water upstairs for bathing — one bucket per person.

The small room had a six-by-six-inch mirror, the only one in the house. There Tapo and Emily could do their hair or Emily might apply some eye makeup. I had a tiny mirror in my lipstick container and used only that. I found it a relief not to encounter my own reflection every time I used the bathroom or walked into my bedroom. I became less concerned about my hair and almost stopped wearing makeup.

Downstairs was a large walled courtyard where Mommy and Daddy slept on two hemp cots brought out in the evening. They covered each with a frame holding up mosquito netting. From above they looked like two white mummies. Uncle must have slept in one of the unfurnished rooms around the courtyard. Whether they had no furniture because of poverty or termites, I am unsure. Termites attacked any wood, even burrowing into the frames Emily had around pictures of Babaji, Ramana Maharshi, and Jesus. The kitchen had the barest essentials—a gas stove, a few dishes, pans, and cutlery. Two gates, like those one might find on a warehouse, opened onto a pathway that connected the main street, the Parikrama Marg, to the Yamuna River.

This pathway provided endless entertainment for me because of the people and animals who walked by. Some used the field between us and the river for a toilet. At least once or twice a day, a man or male youth would arrive carrying a pot of water. Indians consider toilet paper unsanitary and clean themselves with water. Women, their saris serving as cover, sometimes would squat just beyond our dwelling, but I never saw a woman with a water pot.

Mommy liked it when cows came by, especially if they left a manure pile. She would collect the leavings and use her hands to make flat pies, about the size of a small frisbee. Then she plastered them on the outside wall of the house to dry out. One of the neighbors conducted a small business selling dung pies. There was no need to worry about stepping in cow manure when walking on the path; enterprising women picked it up before it even cooled.

These dung pies became the fuel for cooking *chapattis*, the flatbread most Indians eat daily. Mommy had retired from regular cooking, leaving that chore to Tapo or Uncle, but she still made

Uncle, Mommy, and Tapoguna. Uncle and Mommy are browning chapattis over a dung fire.

chapattis with Uncle every day. She sat on the floor, cross-legged, rolling out the dough, and Uncle squatted while cooking. They built a dung fire in a small unit resembling a hibachi grill and proceeded to cook, then brown, the flatbread over the fire. Since Indians rarely eat with utensils, the *chapattis* also serve as an instrument to pick up the rice, dal, and vegetables that make up their diet.

At dusk, one neighbor came out to the path with a long stick that had the electric wire from the house attached to it. Somehow he would hook up that wire to the main wire, and *voila*, the lights to his house came on. By the time I awoke in the morning, the connecting wire always had been taken down. These people, who will hardly kill a fly, didn't hesitate to steal electricity off the grid.

Vrindavan is in Krishna country. According to the stories, the deity grew up and performed his heroic feats in the nearby hills. The International Society for Krishna Consciousness (ISKCON) that spawned the Hari Krishnas is located downtown. Because this is a holy place, one cannot openly buy meat, alcohol, or mouse poisoning, as I later found out.

I visited ISKCON often because the Internet business I used to e-mail letters home was a half block away, and the center had decent public restrooms. Krishna worshippers from all over the world congregated there for classes or to visit the tomb of their founder, A. C. Bhaktivedanta Swami

Prabhupada. Many local people also worship Krishna and/or Radha, his consort.

One would think that a town flooded with Westerners eager to dance for Krishna might be clean. The immediate space around the temple was beautifully tiled, but just beyond the gates the dust from a too-worn road made breathing unpleasant. Also, starting just a few blocks away, stacks of rubbish lined the streets. Any beggar can be paid a pittance to sweep the streets and deliver the refuse to these piles. Holy cows stand around the edge, checking for an edible morsel and occasionally eating a plastic bag. Pigs and dogs, both allowed to breed freely, rifle through these stacks and eat anything they can. The rubbish stacks, plastic and all, are later burned, emitting a smell of dirt and smoke and God knows what else into the air. Evidently Krishna consciousness does not yet include environmental consciousness.

One morning I awoke to shouts of "Krishna, Krishna," followed by "Radha, Radha." I looked out and saw a horde of people marching on the Parikrama Marg, a six-mile road that circumnavigates Vrindavan. It is considered a "holy" walk so many people traverse it barefoot. On auspicious days some prostrate themselves, going down first on their knees, then into a full-length supplication, stretching their hands out as far as possible, and placing a rock in front of them to mark the place where the next prostration would begin. Some days groups of forty or fifty people would walk by.

But on that one particular morning, there were hundreds of people. They carried flags and noise-makers but mostly shouted, "Krishna, Krishna" and the response, "Radha, Radha." When I looked closer, I realized the group consisted mostly of young people. In Vrindavan there are no sports or other activities in the schools and no movie theaters. Often, I saw small boys in pickup cricket games in the dusty open areas, sometimes with a proper bat but more often with just a stick. It was the only activity I saw for children. Entertainment at all levels was minimal. Many families owned a small black and white television, although Tapo and Emily did not. As was the norm, they owned only a few books and did not have a radio or any magazine or newspaper subscriptions.

Young married couples rode their scooters to the temples in the evening, said a few prayers, visited with others, and left. In the march for Krishna and Radha, though, the young men and women were yelling for their gods. They all looked happy and excited. It reminded me of a pep rally preceding a high school football game.

When I went to Tapo and Emily's ashram, I assumed there would be a daily schedule of meditation, but Tapo did not regularly meditate. Nor were there any representations of gods, as are found in most Indian homes, save for Emily's pictures. She, a serious seeker, performed a daily ritual with a *mala*, saying a mantra, or prayer, as each bead passed through her fingers. A few days after I arrived, Tapo gave me a mantra to use in my meditations. Disappointed by the lack of structure, I fell into my own daily schedule that included meditation and study of *A Course in Miracles*.

Filling up that emptiness at the center of my being became one focus in my meditations. Sometimes I'd picture that emptiness as a deep ravine in the earth that I would try to fill with dirt. Often, I'd imagine Tapo helping me. I would try to recall all the devastating events—Grandma leaving, Gary leaving, Charlie and his daughter leaving me in the car, Lynette and Daddy leaving me out—to see if there were any bad feelings left. I wanted to use this large amount of time to heal these long-standing wounds, or, as Ken Wapnick might say, let go of my abandonment script.

Tapoguna Maharaj became my other focus. He kept no regular schedule for anything, except making tea for Emily and me each morning. In fact, most days he did very little, reminding me of the ease of my parents. He enjoyed visiting, cooking, napping, or just sitting. What a contrast to the hard-charging people I admired in the United States.

Emily, Tapo, and I did take a walk most evenings. He owned only one pair of shoes. They were made of black cloth and were slightly too big for him. I offered to buy him a new pair, but he indicated he didn't need any. "I can walk all day in these shoes," he said. "My feet never hurt because I have no tension."

When I returned to India the following year, we met for a trip, including a visit to Gangotri near the Chinese border, where the faithful visit an auspicious temple and walk to the mouth of the Ganges. The water there pours from a glacier, but many take a ritual dunk despite the cold. Most people make the pilgrimage in three days, walking on the first day into the foothills of the Himalayas to an ashram where they receive free food and a blanket. On day two, they go to the mouth of the Ganges and return to the ashram for a second night. They walk back to Gangotri on the third day. Young walkers sometimes skip the second night at the ashram and come straight back. Wearing those same cloth shoes, Tapo walked the entire trip and back in one long day.

One evening as we walked, I asked Tapo about his enlightenment. The three of us sat on a grassy mound overlooking the Yamuna River. The scene was pleasant but not beautiful because everything I saw in India looks dirty, worn, or both. The grass where we sat had been chewed down to the dirt by wandering cows. The river was a dirty brown and the air, filled with smog, smelled of industry and filth. Tapo said when he was eight or nine he began going to hear holy men by himself. His parents were from the Kshatriya caste of warriors and leaders, born out of the arms of Brahman and not particularly religious.

After college, Tapo traveled and walked about, as spiritual aspirants in India tend to do. Looking for teachers, he visited gurus. He went, among other places, to Babaji's ashram in Gujarat where he met Emily. He began his serious spiritual work in Rishikesh, a town known for its spiritual teachers and ashrams and the place where the Beatles spent time at the ashram of the late Maharishi Mahesh Yogi, the founder of Transcendental Meditation. Tapo lived in a cave for six months, meditating constantly, almost never sleeping.

Later, he went to Allahabad to a *mela*, a big spiritual gathering, and was eating a meal when a dam in his mind broke. "You know how God just drips, drips, drips into your mind when you are meditating," he said. "All of a sudden, it wasn't a drip, it was a flood of God." The experience, he said, almost deranged him. He laughed for days, perhaps because his perception of the world had changed. Someone at the *mela* told him he had to stop or the authorities would lock him up, but he didn't. Still laughing, he went home to his parents in Vrindavan where his mother found a holy man called Satguru. This man took Tapo under his wing, calmed him down, and gave him his spiritual name. Tapo considered Satguru his guru, even

though he did not meet him until after his enlightenment.

What does it mean to be enlightened? Maybe to
see the world totally differently from the rest of us.
Or to have no reaction to it. Maybe to live in perfect
peace in the midst of pain, violence, and death. A
Course in Miracles says the world is an illusion.
Tapo used to say, "It is all illusion, delusion." I
wondered if he really did experience the world that
way. But how could I be sure he was enlightened?
I wasn't, but I watched him every day for two
months. What I saw impressed me.

Devotees occasionally came to see him while I
was there. One walked for several days to spend a
half hour at Tapo's feet and ask him questions.
Tapo told me I could wake him up at any time
during the night if I wanted something.

"I am never asleep, he said. "My body may be,
but I am not."

Most days he acted like everyone else: he ate,
slept, and cooked. But small things showed me he
functioned at a level beyond me. Once, I encountered him with only a cloth wrapped around his
groin as I walked into the small room to enter the
bathroom. I was embarrassed; he was not. The
things in life that disturb us ordinary souls did not
seem to affect him at all.

His father became ill. Tapoguna sat beside him
the first night, playing a harmonium and singing

quietly. The next morning a health care person—not a doctor—came and determined Daddy needed an Ayurvedic medicine. When any of us went to town, we did so either in the morning or evening because it was almost one hundred degrees in the middle of the day. The family owned no mode of transportation, not even a bicycle. Emily and I always caught a rickshaw at the end of the path on the Parikrama Marg for the two-mile ride into town. When Tapo heard what his father needed, he walked all the way to town right in the middle of the day. Returning, he happily gave over the medicine, seemingly unconcerned about the heat or his father's condition. He had done his duty and appeared prepared to accept the outcome. Later, when it got cold in the evenings, he wore exactly the same clothes.

On one evening outing Tapo wanted Emily and me to see some ruins. We walked a long way to reach them. I had to sit down because my back and legs ached. Emily also had difficulty because of her weight. As we sat on the steps of the ruins, I said to Tapo, "It is too bad you are saddled with us older people. It really slows you down."

"It is as it should be," he replied without hesitation. "I am young. You are older. I can take care of you." After resting, we caught a boat to go on the Yamuna River, the better to see the full length of the ruins. Tapo talked to the boatman before we rowed out. When we returned, I asked how much money I should pay. Tapo told me, and I paid. The boatman then asked for more. They spoke Hindi, of course, so Tapo had to report the conversation to me later. Tapo spoke to him respectfully but refused to give him any more money. He said that we'd made an agreement about the price before we started and that, if the boatman had wanted more, he should have said so at that time and we would have decided whether we wanted to pay that amount. Emily said Tapo never passed up an opportunity to give a teaching.

At one point, my room became infested with mice. At first, I saw just one or two when they scurried across the room. Then, they ran across my bed at night and even up my pants as I sat in my plastic chair, making it difficult to maintain meditative concentration. They must have liked something in my suitcase, perhaps the cough drops I'd brought from home because I often found mice dirt in the suitcase with my clothes.

The family, being good Hindus who killed nothing, had a solution. In the evening they put food in a bucket and devised a way for the mice to get into it. Once inside, the mice could not get out. Uncle would take out the bucket the next morning and dump the mice in the field across the path. That method, however, did not reduce the mouse population in my room, so I decided to buy some mice and rat poison. Not an easy task because most shopkeepers near ISKCON would not carry it.

Several shopkeepers recommended I go to the market on the other side of town, but we rarely went there. Finally, I found an enterprising shopkeeper who kept some hidden behind the counter. Once I bought it, though, I didn't have enough nerve to use it without Tapo's permission.

One day I discovered a mouse had eaten through the zipper on my suitcase, making it impossible for me to close it properly. That did it. Tapo decided something had to be done, and I confessed I already owned some poison.

"Can I use it?" I asked him.

"I will tell you in the morning," he replied. Then he did a quick meditation, as if consulting someone or some other part of himself. Ten minutes later, he said, "Yes, you can poison them."

That night I put out a little poison in just two places and had planned to repeat the process the next night. But I never saw another mouse, dead or alive. I wondered if the poison had killed them, or if Tapo magically had told them all to leave.

Emily, Tapo, and I took two trips while I was there, the first to Rishikesh, two hundred miles north of Delhi. We went in an overnight bus, making for one of the most hellish nights of my life. My bunk, reminiscent of an overhead compartment in an airplane, was the farthest forward, just across from the driver, who played high-pitched Indian music all night to keep him awake. He also opened a window; the breeze cooled him and froze me. Additionally, we hit a pothole at least every minute, jarring my back against the metal of the bunk. Though no one cooked, the smell of curry from the food the locals brought with them, or just from their clothes, permeated the bus.

At eight in the morning we arrived in Haridwar, about ten miles from Rishikesh. It was the last stop for that bus. Tapo got off, happy as a schoolboy who had just won a prize. He couldn't wait to show Emily and me the spot on the Ganges where Hindus had gathered for the Kumbh Mela, a grand religious event occurring every three years. I couldn't focus on *melas*, even the big one. My head throbbed from no caffeine, and my bladder from no restroom. Tapo had no addictions and could hold his urine for a very long time. I complained about the ride. He'd slept like a baby, though he and Emily had shared a narrow double bunk.

We stayed a few days in Rishikesh, visiting his old haunts, including the cave he lived in during his intense meditation. I checked out places to stay if I decided to return. On our way home we booked a 5:00 a.m. train from Haridwar and stayed in a hotel across the street from the station. Emily and Tapo had a television in their room. Tapo, who had not seen much television in his life, watched it all night long, but the next morning he acted no differently than if he had eight hours of sleep. Second-class trains have only hard bunks on which to sleep, but that didn't bother him. He slept much of the twelve-hour ride back to Vrindavan. He didn't eat that day and made no show about his fast. His lack of concern about drinking, eating, sleeping, or peeing made a big impression on me. I couldn't be happy unless I responded to the demands of my body; his didn't seem to have any.

On our second trip we went to the Punjab, where people wanted Tapo to give some teachings. They weren't devotees, just admirers of his spiritual gifts. Punjabis carry the Indian tradition of hospitality to the extreme: his admirers had an entire program of activities and meals planned for us. The first evening an assigned host family asked us to come for food. Tapo said he didn't care to eat, which created a big fuss. Everyone was speaking in Hindi or Punjabi, but I kept hearing the word "snan" being bandied about. I asked Emily what transpired.

"Maharaj (that is what she called Tapo) always bathes before he eats," Emily whispered, reminding me that many Hindus follow this custom. I knew Tapo bathed every morning and often had seen him washing in the afternoon; that must have been what he was doing when I caught him almost nude. But I didn't realize that he refused to eat unless he bathed.

At last I understood why he didn't eat on the train. But I couldn't believe he was taking this position, especially with Punjabis.

"Washing or bathing is part of physical form. It can't be that critical," I said to him. "Anything physical is part of the illusion."

Becoming more flustered than I'd seen him in any other situation, he responded, "If we didn't wash before we eat, we would be like animals, like monkeys."

I felt my anger rise. Why anger, I am not sure. Maybe it was that repressed anger Dr. Sarno said I had. I felt betrayed because I thought we agreed, at least in theory, that physical life was illusion. I wanted to add what was in my mind: *If we have to wash before we eat, the next step might be that we must wear a turban. Soon we have an entire set of rules that sets one group off from another. We then would have different religions that can fight each other for each group's perception of truth.* But I was hesitant to teach the teacher.

He made a friendly comment to me that melted my anger and did give up his bath, settling for washing his hands and arms. That event made me think that gurus don't live in an enlightened state at all times and that they, like ordinary humans, are influenced by culture.

One other small incident reinforced that belief. Tapo was a joyful person, especially on our daily walks. One evening back in Vrindavan we were walking on the bridge across the river, watching the ever-intriguing line of traffic — from camel-driven carts to trucks, constructed from kits, with an engine in front and a homemade bed behind. I brought my camera and wanted to take Tapo's picture because Emily's photographs all showed him with a serious expression. I wanted a shot of that boyish, joking face I saw every day, but as soon as I started snapping, he refused to smile and became a serious religious figure. Other gurus, like Ramana Maharshi and Satya Sai Baba, mostly have controlled countenances in their pictures. Maybe Indians expect their saints to look serious.

I wanted Tapo to be beyond the limits of culture. I was annoyed he still carried habits of Indian society, which perhaps said more about me than him. But these two events made me wonder what it meant to be enlightened. *Maybe one cannot live in a heightened state all of the time, but perhaps Tapo and other gurus could return to that state through meditation.* I recalled Didi's long periods of morning meditation before she met devotees in Calcutta. Whether Tapo occasionally fell into cultural habits dimmed his light in my eyes only slightly. Living with him cheek by jowl for two months made me see how far I had to go to reach enlightenment.

CHAPTER 13

Rishikesh, 2006

After one day in Rishikesh, with four months to go, anxiety spread through me. It started in the bottom of my stomach and crept up to my heart, even impeding my breath. Standing in my bleak hotel room in the business section, I knew meditating would be impossible in that state. I had to find a way to settle myself.

I had returned to India at the beginning of February without a plan or even a reservation. After I walked out of the Delhi Airport to the dark night to negotiate the price for a taxi—something I always do in India—I gave the driver instructions to an inexpensive hotel near the railroad station. I found the one where Emily, Tapo, and I had stayed just before I left in the fall. I operated with clear purpose—to get to Rishikesh for what I hoped would be the culmination of my long spiritual search.

The name Rishikesh means "hair of the rishis," those wise men who gave the original teachings of the Vedas, the scriptures on which a large part of Hindu teachings are based. The rishis went beyond the mundane world to intuit truth. Spiritual seekers from all over the world as well as India flock to Rishikesh in hopes of having a spiritual breakthrough. They want to experience non-duality or perfect peace or receive a blessing from an enlightened person.

Before I got to Rishikesh I knew I'd have to stay a day in Delhi because getting a train ticket might not be easy. At that time all tickets had to be bought at the train station. Sometimes, as I found out returning from the Punjab with Tapo and Emily, one had to fight through crowds to get a ticket. On that trip I'd had to buy the tickets because the women's line had only about twenty people in it, as opposed to the men's line, two hundred long, where Tapo would have to go. Emily did not do tickets or lines. When I got to the front of the line, the ticket mistress did not just hand me the tickets: she wrote out in slow motion each of our names on our individual tickets. I wasn't about to suffer through that again.

So I went to the concierge at a slightly more upscale hotel than the one where I was staying and paid a young man fifty rupees to stand in line for my ticket. The next day I hired another to go with me to the station and get my bags on the correct train. Almost immediately, after I got on a commuter train to Haridwar, I began talking with Pradeep, a young engineer going to Rishikesh to start up some equipment in a plant owned by his company. We got on so well that he invited me to be his guest in the cab from Haridwar to Rishikesh and then have dinner with him and his fellow engineers at the hotel where we all stayed. They made me feel so comfortable, as if I were someone their own age, instead of the age of their mothers. But the next day they went to work.

I'd felt at ease coming to India this time, so confident about finding a hotel in Delhi and getting to Rishikesh. But once I was there, all confidence left me. I began to question the entire enterprise.

Rishikesh, located in the foothills of the Himalayas, is built in three main sections—one business and two religious—along both banks of the Ganges. The religious sections are made up of more than two hundred ashrams, along with shops, restaurants, and guesthouses. All the buildings cluster around two walking bridges about a mile apart, Ram Jhula and Laxman Jhula, named for the heroic brothers of the *Ramayana*, one of two great Hindu myths, the other being the *Mahabharata*, of which the *Bhagavad Gita* is a part. I caught a motorized rickshaw as far as it would go—only motorcycles go over the bridges—to Ram Jhula and walked through the main section of ashrams to a hotel near where Emily, Tapo, and I had stayed previously. I rented a room and moved my belongings from the other hotel with the help of an old man with a cart especially designed to transport bags across the bridges. I settled into the Brijwasi Palace, a typical Indian (as opposed to Western) hotel. It was no palace.

Early the next morning I woke to the familiar pounding in my head. The chill in the air—there was no heater, of course—made me want to stay in bed, but the desire for caffeine, especially in the form of wonderful Indian tea, made me toss off the covers and pull on as many clothes as I could. The restaurant in the Green Hotel, the main haunt for Westerners in this part of town, had not yet opened at that early hour. Nor had the tea wallah just around the corner so I walked to the street parallel to the Ganges. The air smelled fresh because there was little pollution that close to the mountains. The light of the just-rising sun hit this street first, so I enjoyed the heat it brought. Finally, I found a tea cart opening up for morning customers. The operators of these stands make tea one cup at a time. They boil the tea in water, pour in milk and a lot of sugar—I always asked for half the regular amount—and sometimes ginger or cardamom. Then they boil the concoction again. Lastly, they strain the tea into a glass. What a wonderful product, and all for about a dime.

That morning, a few beggars who had slept in the street began to rouse themselves. One man, wearing a black coat, lay against a mostly black cow and a black dog. I had to look hard, as none had yet moved, to perceive where the animals ended and the man began. Soon the line of beggars and *sadhus* (wandering yogis or monks), each carrying his stainless steel begging bowl, began to form against the walls of the buildings. They also were enjoying the sun's warmth. Every day one of the ashrams gives out free food — rice, dal, and vegetables — to all takers. The food arrives in buckets, and volunteers ladle it into individual containers, enough for each person to survive the day. Yet many persons don't accept the food and keep on begging. I wondered if they didn't like the ashram fare, which looked the same every day, or if they just wanted money. Most beggars seemed desperate, but some women, often with a baby, beg in order to bring in a second income.

After enjoying two teas and toast, I walked down the street. One ashram had built a structure that extended into the Ganges: it featured a big, white statue of Shiva. Cows wandered the street at will, including an occasional Brahma bull with horns and the standard hump on its neck. I even met cows on the bridge. Once I saw one eat popcorn out of a bag a woman held at her side. The kiosks began opening and playing sacred music. The air started to fill with strains of "Om nah mah Shiva; Shiva om nah mah."

Settling into a hotel hadn't diminished my anxiety though. Over the next few days I located shops that offered Internet services and yoga classes, which also were held at many hotels and ashrams. I tried to meditate, but I couldn't even do my daily reading of *A Course in Miracles*. Mostly, I hung out at the Green Hotel restaurant, trying to find Westerners to talk to and confirming, I suppose, April Moon's statement that my own company was inadequate. For a few wonderful days, I hooked up with Judy, an Australian woman, and her twelve-year-old son. The boy's father owned a nightclub, but his real money came from serving as a courier for a drug organization. Unfortunately for the boy, his father got caught and, because he wouldn't tell for whom he worked, he was serving a ten-year jail sentence. The boy began having difficulty in school, so his mother decided to take him traveling for six months. They'd already been to Sikkim and to Goa but now seemed at loose ends. She, too, was looking for company.

Judy, a natural beauty, had spent most of her life seeking men and even had acquired a new set of breasts to assist her. But, like me, she had altered her search and refocused on God. Even her half-inch-long hair, cut in a monk-like style, didn't hide her beauty. We discovered that the Green Hotel offered yoga classes in the afternoons and began taking them together.

An English couple, escaping his one and her two children to go on vacation, joined us for a few days, as did Tapo and Emily, whom I had called as soon as I arrived. The Englishman led us in tai chi before breakfast and Judy and Emily read our Tarot cards later, Emily's expertise being the better of the two.

One day we decided to climb a mountain north of Laxman Jhula and agreed to meet at 9:30 a.m. at the Green Hotel. Emily came but said Tapo was in deep meditation. Finally, we persuaded Emily to bring him back to the present. He hurried into the hotel, she insisting that he eat before venturing forth. In typical Indian fashion, we left about an hour late.

As much as I enjoyed the outings with Tapo and Emily and my new friends from Australia and England, I kept asking myself, *Did you come to India to spend pleasant days with other travelers?* I decided to move to an ashram because I seemed incapable of imposing discipline on myself, so I went to a bookstore run by a man in a Western suit. I thought maybe he could size me up, so I asked what ashram he thought would be best for me.

At his recommendation I checked out two, Sivananda and Yoga Niketan, both on the opposite side of ashram row. I hired the man with the cart to move me back across Ram Jhula into Yoga Niketan, which had lovely gardens with many flowers, including oleander and bougainvillea, and almost no garbage. It also had many aggressive monkeys that stole more than one banana from me, once right from my hand. The rooms, accommodating about seventy-five guests, were nicer and cleaner than those at Sivananda. The benches along the edge of Yoga Niketan also had a view of the Ganges and the ashrams built along the opposite bank.

My room, actually half a duplex, had a desk, a single bed, a closet with pegs instead of a rod, and a semiprivate bathroom with a shower and Western toilet. After staying with Tapo and Emily, it felt positively luxurious. I even shared a porch with whoever stayed in the adjoining room.

Yoga Niketan, which at the time cost nine dollars a day for food, lodging, and yoga classes, posted a strict schedule: the wake-up bell rang (and rang and rang) at 4:30 a.m., followed by meditation and yoga for two-and-a-half hours before breakfast. At five in the afternoon the process began again. They served three meals a day, dinner at eight. The British habit of afternoon tea also prevailed and was served before yoga in the afternoon. The ashram locked its gates at nine. Except for the emphasis on hatha yoga, this schedule was not too different from what I'd read about Christian monastic life and what I'd experienced in the Zen monastery. For the first month I followed the schedule precisely because I wanted the benefit of a discipline. I also wanted to follow the rules, recalling how the Zen Buddhists had corrected me. But I soon found that Indian rules, unlike Japanese rules, are meant to be broken.

My first suitemate was Ben, a young Israeli who didn't pay any attention to the schedule except for the meals. He never went to meditation and only sometimes to yoga. He smoked, although only in his room, which is absolutely against the rules. One morning I saw a young woman leave his room, an offense that later caused another couple to be banned from the ashram. Ben, about twenty-three with dark, curly hair and a heavy beard, had just been discharged from the Israeli army. He said that many Israelis, himself included, feel so disoriented when they find themselves alive and out of the army that they go on big trips, many to India, before deciding about university and the future. Other travelers told me they'd encountered Israelis in Pushkar and Varanasi. At first it annoyed me that he came to an ashram and wouldn't follow the rules, but after hearing his story, I softened my feelings. I had no idea what he had experienced.

My physical problems with sitting confronted me immediately when I first walked into the dimly lit meditation hall, which was strewn with grayish pads and cushions. There were no straight lines like there were in the Zendo. Almost every person present could sit in lotus or half-lotus position. I sat in a chair, but it was hard and my back began hurting within ten minutes. For the next session I tried bringing my yoga blocks and sitting with my legs under me. My back still hurt. Finally, I settled on sitting on a blanket with my back to the wall and my legs half crossed in front of me. In that position I usually could get into a good meditative state for twenty minutes. When I saw that many of the young people didn't come to morning meditation, I began building a case for myself, serving as both prosecutor and defender.

In the morning, I hardly had time for a cup of tea between the wake-up bell and meditation, which began at 5:00 a.m., and I disliked meditating for an hour with a caffeine headache coming on. But even worse was the swami. Most ashrams have several swamis in residence, some of whom give teachings either at their formal meditations or at a *satsang* that also might include music and chanting. Some, like the Sivananda ashram, had many swamis, but some did not speak English and played more ceremonial roles. I began disliking our swami the second day, mainly because he didn't seem to be one of the great souls I'd come to Rishikesh to encounter. Every day my case for not participating grew more substantial: He had a heavy accent and talked mainly about esoteric beliefs in Hinduism, sometimes about the alignment of the stars. He also talked a long time, sometimes for twenty minutes. I wanted silence. In my mind he was guilty as charged, so I began to stay in my room, drinking tea at my leisure, reading my daily lesson from *A Course in Miracles,* and meditating in my own chair.

For another couple of weeks I continued going to the afternoon meditation, but then I realized how lovely it was to sit on the benches at the border of the ashram and watch the *arti,* a ceremony performed every night by the ashram that had erected the statue of Shiva. *Arti,* meaning "offering," began with a group of boys, trainees of the ashram, all dressed in orange, chanting and singing. Drummers kept the beat on *tablas* and other percussion instruments. It ended with the faithful putting a candle on a leaf and sending it down the river. It lasted just as long as the evening meditation. Listening to the music waft across the water and seeing the tiny lights float down the river was more satisfying than hearing the swami.

One night, I went across the river with other Westerners from the ashram to participate in the ceremony. We had difficulty getting a seat close enough to see the boys singing and drummers drumming because of the huge crowd. Putting my little candle in the water at the end did not provide me with the satisfaction it apparently gave the Indians, so I became content to watch from our own ashram.

About eighty brightly colored mats covered most of the floor of the large hall where we held our hatha yoga classes. Morning and evening, young men with degrees in yogic science led us through a series of exercises and relaxation techniques. The sessions resembled classes in the United States though they included more mantras and breath work. When I first arrived, Vishnu, who had brought a group from Canada for teacher training, led the entire group once a day. He had twice won the All-India Yoga Championship competition. Who in America would even know such a contest existed? Amit, another experienced teacher, put us through our paces, usually for a full hour and a half. Unfortunately, he left to teach in Singapore.

Goroff spent more time than anyone on breath work; his classes often didn't last an hour. Yoga teachers often walk around a class and make corrections in students' poses by moving an arm or leg into a better position. These teachers would correct the men around me, but they never touched me. I asked Goroff why. "We cannot touch any female," he said. "That is the rule of the ashram." The rules, established by the founder many years ago, had not been modernized.

Another incident showed me how strict the Indians there could be. I had made friends with David, my second suitemate, and Matthew, a dark South Indian, both in their forties. We appealed to each other because we were serious "older" people who liked to talk about serious issues. The administrator of the ashram once walked by our porch and saw Matthew there. He came over and said in no uncertain terms, "Go to your own room. This is an ashram, and men don't sit and talk with women." No matter that I was old enough to be Matthew's mother.

I stayed at Yoga Niketan for more than three months. Most guests, who averaged about thirty years of age, stayed one to three weeks. The main ethnic group was Japanese. The founder of Yoga Niketan had been to Japan several times and established connections there. In addition, many Japanese travel guides recommended the place. I made friends with one young Japanese man who had just graduated college and landed a job. Anticipating he would work sixteen hours a day for the next ten years, he wanted to meditate to prepare his mind.

Many young people used the ashram as an inexpensive hotel with a built-in community. Others had their own peculiar reasons for being there. One eighteen-year-old man from Korea, whose face was distorted in that both sides did not match, wanted to learn yoga well enough to teach it to Korean girls interested in the physical exercise to maintain their figures. He hoped to get a girlfriend in the process. A thirty-nine-year old Taiwanese dancer, who had the most developed feet and toes I've ever seen, wanted to retool as a yoga teacher. A Finnish yoga instructor came to refine her teaching techniques.

But many were true spiritual seekers. One young woman from Belgium worked in restorative justice and wanted to know herself better before she tried to help others. A European woman decided to read through the Hindu classics and began with the Vedas—a tough slog. I doubt she got too far in the two or three weeks she stayed. A translator from Turkey spent the entire day between breakfast and evening yoga classes in the library reading books written by the Yoga Niketan founder. One German woman in her fifties went all over town looking for the best yoga teachers and studied "techniques" to help her advance her spiritual experiences. She discovered the urine-for-health books and began drinking her own urine while at the ashram.

Much like me, Maria from Germany, who had written books on *pranayama* (techniques of the breath) and who led yoga retreats, wanted support for her own meditation. I liked spending time with her not only because of her knowledge and experience, but also because, like me, she enjoyed eating sweets at the Greek bakery in Laksman Jhula and swimming in the Ganges.

CHAPTER 14

The Wisdom of the Himalayan Masters

I n addition to my own reading and meditating, I began looking for great souls to see or hear. I found one at Sivananda Ashram—Swami Muktananda (not the founder of Siddha Yoga, who died in 1982). He taught each weekday morning until late March, when he flew off to an ashram in France. Swami Muktananda, a big, brown-skinned man who might like his chapattis a tad too much, hid his stomach under a light orange smock. He had that easy way I had come to expect from persons who no longer have axes to grind. Acceptance oozed from his large body.

He spoke in English at 8:30 a.m. and in French at 10:00 a.m. I often ate breakfast at one of the little restaurants near his ashram to make his class on time. Often all chairs were filled before the start time. Swami had been born in Canada to a Haitian father and French Canadian mother. One day he told us that he had wanted to be a monk since he was eleven years old, but because someone had to support his mother, he felt obligated to attend to his filial responsibilities first. He started a business, made what he considered enough money, turned the business over to his brother, and returned to his goal of becoming a monk. In one talk he emphasized the difference between needing money and wanting money. He "needed" money for his mother, he said, but he did not want it.

I particularly liked Swami Muktananda because he didn't let an entourage of special followers form around him. Some devotees followed him to France in March or April when it got too hot in Rishikesh, but he treated everyone who came to his teaching the same way. No personality cult formed around him. Several times he lectured on *moksha*, liberation, saying we are all waves on the ocean, rising up for our experience of individuality.

"There you are, a wave, interested in the looks of your wave or in other waves," he said one day.

"'Hi, wave over there!' But what is important is the ocean. You must become part of it. But you won't look at the ocean."

Another day he said, "You can try to be a good wave, a love-your-neighbor wave, but that is what you are — a wave. If you want to be more, you have to open up to the ocean."

Another favorite topic was free will. Almost every week, someone would ask directly, "Do we have free will?" But even if no one asked, it seemed the question would emerge from another discussion. Swami Muktananda answered the question in various ways. Once he said, "No, we do not have free will. The point of the *Bhagavad Gita* is to show that we have no free will." Another time he declared, "Yes, we have choice, the choice to continue on the path of desire and suffering or to awaken by turning inward. Our lives are like a DVD, and if we continue on the path of desire and suffering, we play the long version, but as we move closer to the Infinite, we can skip tracks on the disc." In that respect he sounded just like Ken Wapnack explaining *A Course in Miracles.*

When a student asked the swami what could be done with all the negativity he experienced, Swami said, "Meditate." I wanted to shout out, "*A Course in Miracles* would say, 'Forgive.'" In fact, I asked Swami Muktananda after class if he considered forgiveness important. He indicated it was, and added "but not as important as meditation."

Shanti Mayi, an American woman who studied with her guru near Laxman Jhula for thirteen years before her enlightenment, held a *satsang* two or three afternoons a week in a large hall at her guru's ashram. Her devotees sat on the floor around a chair reserved for her. Many stayed in guesthouses around Laxman Jhula, some for the entire time she resided in Rishikesh—December to April. Several even left containers filled with clothes and personal effects so they did not have to lug so many bags back and forth from Italy, Australia, America, France, or wherever else they lived. One European devotee had been a follower of Rajneesh, called Osho in India, the guru who caused all the fuss in Oregon for promoting free love (to see how empty it was) and possessing numerous Rolex watches and Rolls-Royce automobiles (gifts from devotees). When Rajneesh died in 1990, the devotee switched to Shanti Mayi.

That first day I found a chair and placed it with those of other chair-sitters in the back of the crowd. Someone played a harmonium, someone else a guitar. We sang a song, referring to the words passed around on a sheet of paper. Though the faithful participated in the music, they really wanted Shanti Mayi.

A curtain separated the room in half, and she entered through the empty part of the room. The audience knew by some signal when she would enter so everyone was standing in reverence by the time she made her appearance. A woman in her fifties, she wore a loose dress and no shoes. She looked to me like a middle-class housewife, mainly because she had dyed her hair a sandy blonde color, but she was a saint to her devotees. Muktananda's followers tended to be *jnana* types, interested in knowledge and understanding. Shanti Mayi's were *bhakti*. They loved her.

Judging from specific references she made in her talks, she apparently knew the personal lives of many of her followers. One Australian woman wondered about some techniques in meditation. Shanti Mayi told her that she worried too much about small things, and that she should quit meditating for a year. "Give it up," she demanded. "Start living from your heart. Stop making plans because the future is unknowable." She used that advice as a segue to speak of her own enlightenment.

"I became self-realized at 2:00 p.m. while working at a vegetable canning plant," she said. "When I checked into work that day, I had no idea what was coming. Even at 1:59, I had no notion. Then at 2:00 p.m. I saw the entire universe in my own mind." Later in that talk she said she does not teach Hinduism, Buddhism, or Christianity. Rather she teaches people to know themselves and be free. "A yogi accepts things exactly the way they are."

I hoped I could remember to act like a yogi the next time I found myself panicky in some tight spot. Maybe then, at some later point, I wouldn't feel any tight spots.

Another time, a man asked what to do about his lust. She gave him a picture of Mary, mother of Jesus, as representative of the feminine, suggesting that he meditate on her face and try to transform lust, which weakens an individual, into love, which strengthens.

A smart young man from Canada asked about how to surrender because he was practicing doing it. "Surrender isn't something you practice," Shanti Mayi replied sharply. "You just do it."

I went to a half dozen of her *satsang*s. Several times we chanted the Medicine Buddha Mantra, which made us part of a worldwide healing circle. The intention was to send healing to anyone needing it. Shanti Mayi states on the Medicine Buddha website:

> *It is a sad time for the world. We must realize that this great illness we experience at this time is not isolated to the USA or the Middle East or even the invisible Terrorists. This illness that is so evident today is rooted way back in time and will continue to reach far into the future until every being comes to the great realization that greed and self-centered hypocrisy is the true enemy of humanity. Wherever it may originate or wherever it may be directed, it is this enemy that we must overcome. So let us begin within*

ourselves. We ourselves are the great medicine for our great illness.

A Course in Miracles, Charlie Brown, Sai Baba, and the Sermon on the Mount say the same thing, albeit in different language.

Shanti Mayi's life again raised the question for me about the relationship of the enlightened person and the world. She had been married and had children before her intense spiritual work. Her second husband, who sat in the back, seemed to manage her business of being a guru: he made arrangements; sold things, like calendars with her sayings on them; and protected her time. She made a comment one day in *satsang* that she wouldn't be traveling so much the next year because of the constraints of money. Swami Muktananda, on the other hand, was a celibate monk who lived in a large ashram with branches all over the world, apparently freeing him personally from money concerns. I felt in no position to judge if one life were more spiritual than the other. Was Shanti Mayi's dyed hair any different from Muktananda's big belly? Did either matter?

I had heard that a one-hundred-two-year-old yogi lived at and still headed Ved Niketan, one of the big ashrams where lots of young people on tight budgets stayed. It was located across the river from Yoga Niketan. I made it a goal to have *darshan* with him. He had a very long name I couldn't remember, but everyone knew who I was referring to when I said "Old Swami." It was a hike to get to his ashram—down our hill, past Sivananda, across Ram Jhula, and down ashram row about a half mile. I went to the desk and asked if he were available. "Sorry, no," said the man, who was dressed in orange.

The next time I went, I persuaded my suitemate David, a forty-year-old psychotherapist from New York, to accompany me. That persuasion wasn't easy because David took no risks. He never ate outside the ashram and would not check out the other teachers or swim in the Ganges. He just wanted to do some yoga, meditate, and get a flavor of India. We arrived just as a crowd of people with name tags around their necks flooded the ashram. I thought that perhaps the Old Swami was going to do something big. Someone yelled, "Swami is coming. Hurry up and take a seat." So we did, along with two hundred other people, all with the same name tags, which read, "The Art of Living." A bearded Indian swami—certainly not the old one—made preliminary remarks and then asked us to divide into groups of eight, all sitting on the floor.

Realizing we did not belong, David and I could have left at that point, but my adventuresome spirit took over. I recalled that crashing an Indian wedding twenty-five years ago hadn't turned out so well, but nothing bad could happen with so many people around. *What fun to participate in someone else's program,* I thought, as I found a group near the back of the room. *Was David also curious or just afraid to walk out of a huge hall?* All I knew was that he followed my lead. After we divided up, the swami announced, "Just as yesterday you shared your everyday fantasies, today you are to share your sexual fantasies." A groan emanated from the participants. A queasy feeling ran through my gut though the activity immediately made sense to me. In coming to complete acceptance of ourselves, we must look at anything about which we might be ashamed. And what creates more shame and guilt than sex? *If we can just keep our cover, we will be all right*, I thought. Surprisingly, no one questioned our lack of name tags.

I could see by David's expression that he felt trapped. To walk out would be too obvious and to talk would be too threatening. "I am not participating," he announced to the group, but by the time his turn came, he did. Many of the shared fantasies were of the garden variety. One man loved big breasts. One woman fantasized about performing oral sex on all the young men at her workplace. But one young man's fantasies were very dark, including incest, violence, and death. Speaking last when everyone wanted to finish up, I revealed only that, as I'd gotten older, my fantasy had moved from the bed to the breakfast table. I'd be satisfied, I said, to have someone to talk to in the morning. At the end of the session David and I left, no one ever discovering we were impostors.

The next time I went to Ved Niketan I got Matthew to accompany me. His being banned from my porch didn't keep us apart. We had an audience with the Old Swami, who received us in a small room while sitting in full lotus and wearing only an orange loincloth. He was very thin but not frail, and his back was as straight as a board. With every breath his belly moved in and out. He did not speak English, so we had to rely on a translator, who showed us photos of the asana show Old Swami put on for devotees on his one-hundredth birthday. At that point he could still do the most difficult yoga poses, including wrapping his leg around his neck.

Swami wore glasses and had false teeth but was otherwise in perfect health. Twice a day he drank a glass of milk boiled with *tulsi*, holy basil. Swami told us he sleeps three hours a night, and then made a joke, "Yogis sleep three hours, regulars six hours, and patients ten hours." He laughed a big guffaw. I couldn't help wondering if he were asking us, "How sick are you?" He intends to live twenty-five more years, because, he said, he has so much he wants to get done at the ashram.

On this Indian trip, I had wanted to make some progress. I wanted to earn an A in spiritual advancement. That's why I left behind the annoyances of everyday life, the family disagreements, and even the nightly news to focus almost all my time on spiritual activities. Fortunately, I did have some powerful experiences — none with a guru.

The first happened in meditation before I stopped going to the meditation hall. I got myself into as comfortable a pose as I could, tried to ignore the swami, and concentrated on my breath. I moved into a deep meditation, unaware when the swami stopped speaking. Before I knew it, the lights came up and the meditation was over. I felt I had experienced a time collapse. I suppose it's possible I went to sleep, even though it did not feel like that either during the meditation or when the lights came on. Having just lost more than a half hour, part of me felt disoriented.

Another experience occurred in a yoga class led by a teacher who often ended the session with a *yoga nidra*, or yogic sleep, in which the leader moves the practitioner's attention from one body part to another, from fingers to wrists to arms, to all parts of the body. This classic hypnotic technique often puts me in an altered state of awareness. One day I felt myself going deeper and deeper into a trance. My entire body, but especially my back, began tingling, as if it wanted to pop off the mat. If the teacher had given the suggestion, I felt sure I could levitate, but he didn't, and I returned to mundane experience.

My biggest experience happened one afternoon, just after tea, when I was alone. I was reading a book about the South Indian saint Ramana Maharshi that had been given to me by one of the Indian women at the ashram. I stopped reading for a moment, closed my eyes, and began a short meditation. A wonderful feeling spread from my heart all through my body, the same feeling that I had meditating with Nirupama that had sent me off on my first trip to India. I often had moments of this feeling during meditation, but as Tapo had said, the feeling just dripped into my consciousness. This time it *was* more like a flood, a feeling of complete oneness with the world, or as Swami Muktananda might say, oneness with the ocean, with the Infinite. Do I daresay it was oneness with God? I wondered if this is what Christians feel when they are "born again" or what nuns and monks of any religion feel after long periods of prayer or meditation, or what Zen Buddhists feel when they have just cracked a *koan*, or what dervishes feel after a spell of twirling.

When I opened my eyes, the feeling did not disappear. Only for a few seconds after sex have I ever had such a feeling with my eyes open. Nearing time to go to yoga, I went to the bathroom and changed clothes. The feeling stayed. I walked, slowly and carefully, so as not to dislodge this fragile state, to the yoga hall. There I found myself next to the young man who later was kicked out of the ashram for sleeping with a woman. I usually thought of him as an egotistic know-it-all, but that day I felt nothing but love for him. As the class wore on, the bliss faded, and I didn't like him so much. I was back in ordinary air.

I believe I had an experience of enlightenment—a long, holy instant as *A Course in Miracles* would call it. I found out before I left the yoga hall that I was not an enlightened person, but now I knew what my goal was—to live with love for every person, not just to say it but also to feel it in my heart. That day I knew that it mattered very little what I believed, whether I called myself a Christian, Buddhist, Muslim, Hindu, a student of *A Course in Miracles*, or a reflective atheist: all paths must ultimately lead to this experience of universal love.

Though I now live more contentedly, I know that before I could exist in that exalted state, I have to forgive myself for many petty peeves and resentments and overcome numerous insecurities and addictions. I hadn't even completely abandoned the thought—the dream—that there might be a man in my future. One of Emily's Tarot card readings said there would be. It's nice to think that a special man would make my life wonderful. But I've had enough experiences to realize I won't find lasting joy and perfect peace with any man or in any land unless I let the deepest part of myself be filled with the source of all life. That's what I call God.

Epilogue

I n the spring of 2012, I attended a Buddhist retreat at which the leader told us to make a *mandala* of our spiritual lives. The word *mandala*, translated from Sanskrit, means circle. In Hinduism and Buddhism *mandalas* appear as sacred paintings. The leader gave us colored sand, construction paper, decorative flowers, colored sequins, scissors, ribbons, and glue.

I began with a green piece of construction paper, and cut out three pink circles to represent the three main spiritual influences of my life. I positioned the circles to form a triangle. Surrounded by Buddhists, I initially wasn't comfortable making a trinity, especially since I placed Jesus at the top and Satya Sai Baba and Buddha at the bottom. Deciding I was no longer looking for approval, I pasted the circles on the paper and added a flower to each.

Around my three flowers I placed sequins to represent other teachers, especially my grandmother, Ken Wapnack, and April Moon. Then I pasted white clouds at the top to represent enlightenment and black forms along the bottom to represent dark forces still hiding in the iceberg of my subconscious but pricking the surface and expressing themselves in my body. I still get a stomachache if I make a mistake playing bridge. My chest tightens if people make too much noise chomping their food. My shoulders constrict if my granddaughter doesn't finish reading her books for English class.

But maybe that deep emptiness I felt inside me when Grandma and Gary left, and when Charlie and his daughter didn't include me, does have a bottom. My younger daughter and her partner took my sister, Lynette, and her husband and me to see *The Marriage of Figaro* at the Metropolitan Opera House in New York City. Unfortunately, my daughter couldn't get all the tickets for adjacent seats. Someone had to sit alone. Every person volunteered to take the single seat, but I knew both couples would enjoy the opera more if they sat together. So I insisted on taking the single seat with no worry about being left out. When the music began, my heart opened and I felt part of something larger than a couple, larger than our group.

I can't say, as Nirupama did, that I'll never feel lonely again, but at least I've stopped judging myself so severely for not being perfect and, at last, my heart is never empty. My teachers live within me as do three teachings on which they all agree: love everyone, stay present, forgive everything.

Acknowledgments

I thank the people who have made contributions to this work.

My teachers, without whom there would be no story. Kenneth Wapnack led me through *A Course in Miracles* and forced me to apply its teachings to my life. April Moon directed me to plunge deeper into the spiritual life. Satya Sai Baba, through his miracles, changed my view of the physical world. Tapoguna Maharaj showed me a life without the support of material "necessities." Gary Renard, Sheila Reynolds, Zdenko Arsenijevic, and Louise Hay all opened new areas of understanding.

Readers of earlier drafts of this book, who made useful suggestions. Especially helpful were Susan Eddy, Ross Gay, Janet Kamnikar, and my former colleagues Cori Jones, Brock Haussaman, and Tom Valasek. My sister Lynette, who read and reread, jogged my memory and marked pages with her teacher's pen.

My editor and teacher Lorraine Ash, who has been with me every step of the way.

My family members, who were always with me. My late grandmother Vida Mallory Pershall and my late parents Ralph and Gladys Pershall provided the spiritual basis for my life. Gary and Charlie, both of whom I loved and lost, were gateways into a broader world. My children, to whom this book is dedicated, made life meaningful and fun and sustained me through my darkest hours.

About the Author

Myrna J. Smith grew up on a farm in Eastern Oregon, married young, and completed a master's degree before giving birth to three children. During her 34-year career as a professor, she wrote extensively in the field of education. After her midlife divorce, her exploration of the world's religions brought her to India four times. Today she enjoys competitive bridge and continues to travel at every opportunity.

For her next writing project, about the healing power of sound, she hopes to visit Australia and learn about the didgeridoo from the aborigines. She lives in New Jersey.

Visit Myrna online at www.MyrnaJSmith.com.

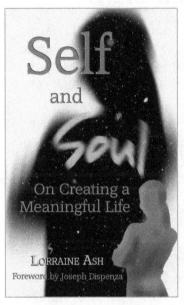

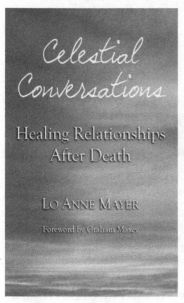

CPSIA information can be obtained
at www.ICGtesting.com
Printed in the USA
LVHW101032060522
718097LV00004B/43